A STRANGER IN THE HOUSE OF GOD

A STRANGER IN THE HOUSE OF GOD

From **Doubt**
to **Faith**
and Everywhere
in Between

JOHN KOESSLER

ZONDERVAN.com/
AUTHORTRACKER
follow your favorite authors

ZONDERVAN®

A Stranger in the House of God
Copyright © 2007 by John Koessler

Requests for information should be addressed to:

Zondervan, *Grand Rapids, Michigan* 49530

Library of Congress Cataloging-in-Publication Data

Koessler, John, 1953–
      A stranger in the house of God : from doubt to faith and everywhere in between /
John Koessler.
            p.   cm.
      Includes bibliographical references.
      ISBN-13: 978-0-310-27413-1
      ISBN-10: 0-310-27413-3
      1. Koessler, John, 1953– 2. Christian biography. I. Title.
BR1725.K585A3   2007
280'.4092 – dc22   [B]

                                                                                    2006037563

Interior design by Beth Shagene

Printed in the United States of America

07 08 09 10 11 12 13 • 22 21 20 19 18 17 16 15 14 13 12 11 10 9 8 7 6 5 4 3 2 1

For Jane,
who lived through some of it,
read all of it,
and always believes I can

Contents

Preface

The block that intersected the street where I grew up was called Church Street. On one end was St. Angela, the Roman Catholic church where most of my friends attended. At the other end was Beulah Baptist, where I first heard the gospel. These two churches marked the boundaries of my earliest spiritual landscape.

My parents were not churchgoing people. Raised by devout Roman Catholic parents, my father was suspicious of the church and embittered by his experience in a parochial school. My mother was more sympathetic toward church, seeing the value it might have for others, but felt no personal need to attend.

With such a background, it's not surprising that I felt out of place when I finally found my way into the congregation. What does come as something of a surprise is that I have remained there. This book describes my spiritual journey from doubt to faith. In it I share what it was like to feel like an unwelcome stranger at the door and to move from there to the pew, the pulpit, and back to the pew again.

Although the congregation has been my calling, it has not always been a comfortable place for me. I wrote this book partly for my sake. It is my attempt to learn from my experience and to understand why, after being an outsider, a visitor, a church member, and a pastor, I still feel like a stranger in the house of God. It is my story, but not mine alone. Over the years, I have discovered many other pilgrims who travel the same path. It is my prayer that as you read my story, you will have a better understanding of your own. I hope you too will see that you are not alone as you travel in the way. More important, I am praying that you will see the guiding hand of God as it leads you on your journey:

> *Through many dangers, toils and snares*
> *we have already come.*
> *T'was Grace that brought us safe thus far*
> *and Grace will lead us home.*

Introduction

Examine nature accurately, but write from recollection,
and trust more to the imagination than the memory.
—Samuel Taylor Coleridge

Coleridge is right to link imagination and recollection.
Remembering is not the same thing as memory. Memory is a photograph. It captures a fact and preserves it. Remembering, on the other hand, is a reflective process. It is more an art than a science.

Many of our experiences are difficult to recall because they are so common. They are too mundane to worry about their preservation. Was she wearing a blue dress or a green one? Were we dating or married? What was his name? The answers to these questions are left to fade from memory the way the words fade from a newspaper that was read once and then cast to the side of the road.

Remembering is the act of "re-collecting" one's thoughts and feelings. When we remember, we recall the past from the shadowy places of the mind. Some "memories" are easy to access, stored in places that are well within our reach. They are worn from use and we bring them out regularly, like the road trip you took with your college buddies the day after graduation or the antics of your best friend on the Fourth of July.

Other recollections are less accessible, like the memory of your child's first step or a bride's shyness on her wedding night. Preserved with love, they have been put on a high shelf where they can be reached only with effort. We bring them out on special occasions

11

like weddings and funerals, handling them with a mixture of care and familiarity, the way a daughter might lay out her mother's china and silverware at Christmas.

Some remembrances, while not entirely beyond recall, are buried deep within a crevice of the mind. They have been cast there in the hope that they will remain hidden, perhaps even lost forever. These are brought back into the light with great difficulty. Like Christ at the tomb of Lazarus, we must call them forth and unwrap them with care, trying not to notice the stink of the grave.

The stories in this book are all "true." That is to say, they recount events that actually happened to me. Some of the names have been changed, and at points dialog has been reconstructed based on my memory of the essence of what was said. It is important to know that these are recollections and not photographic accounts. They accurately represent my perception of what took place. But the events are described as I now see them, especially the stories of my childhood. This means that, while I have tried to recapture what I saw and felt, these accounts have passed through the filter of my present point of view. To that degree they are edited.

The stories of my childhood are not the firsthand accounts of a child but descriptions of the child's point of view as seen through the eyes of the adult that child became. Even my adult experiences take on a different hue in the retelling. I see metaphors and analogies today that may not have been clear to me at the time. Memoir is as much about the present as it is about the past. I do not remember in order to recall who I was; I remember to discover who I have become.

Oscar Wilde complained, "I dislike modern memoirs. They are generally written by people who have either entirely lost their memories, or have never done anything worth remembering." Perhaps I will fare better with you and you will find something in these stories worth remembering. My real hope is that you will see something of yourself in these stories or that they will open your eyes to your own story. When imagination casts its light on the landscape of the past, we find ourselves in familiar but unexplored country. Welcome to mine. Let us travel together for a while.

CHAPTER 1

Church Street

My friends and I are traveling down Church Street in procession, like pilgrims bound for Jerusalem. I am in the third grade at Chippendale Elementary School across the street from St. Angela's church. School has just let out for the summer and my brother, George, with his Dondi grin and tousled hair, is ahead of me. He is a year and a half older and thinks he can beat me if we get into a fight. He is probably right. Whenever we get into an argument, I threaten to punch him but don't have the heart to follow through. My sister, Lynn, a year and a half younger than me, is lost in the crowd. All skinny legs and pin curls, she looks like Baby Sally in the first grade reader. She wants to be like us.

I think I am fat but my mother says I'm just "big boned." My glasses are thick and my hair curly. I am always the last one to be chosen when teams are formed. I have never lived anywhere else.

When we come to the corner where Church Street intersects our block, I pause and peer into the distance. I want to see if I can make out our house at the other end. It is barely a quarter of a mile away. Whenever I come to that corner, I know I am almost home.

St. Angela, the Roman Catholic church where most of my friends attended, was on one end of Church Street. At the other end was Beulah Baptist, the church where I heard the gospel for the first time. These two churches marked the boundaries of my earliest spiritual landscape. St. Angela was twilight cool and dark as mystery, with its statues of Jesus and Mary and its holy smell. Beulah, on the other hand, met in a plain building with pale walls and blond furniture. It did not smell holy. No statue of Jesus could be found in the place. Between the two, St. Angela felt more like a church to me, though I knew I was not supposed to think such things. My father, a lapsed Catholic, did not like St. Angela or any other church. I gleaned what I knew about the church from my friends, Catholic boys from Polish and Italian families, who attended every Saturday night and thought it a chore.

Once in a while I saw the priests in the market or the department store wearing their white collars. They walked with the stiff dignity of a religious procession. I marveled at the way complete strangers greeted them as they walked by. "Hello, Father," they mumbled, affording them the merest glance, as if they thought it might be a sin to look directly upon such creatures in the full light of day. Their reluctance compelled me to stare, wondering what it was about these men that made people so uncomfortable.

The nuns, too, could sometimes be found outside the confines of the church. They traveled in twos or threes, huddled together like bewildered sightseers in need of a guide. Like their brothers the priests, the nuns were often greeted by those who passed by, but with less apparent dread. Perhaps it was the veil they wore and the way they waddled along on thick legs. Something about the nuns made them seem more vulnerable. Things were different inside the church, according to my friends. There the nuns ruled with an iron fist.

On weekends I walked along with my friends as they went to catechism class. Despite their complaints of boredom, I was as jealous of their Catholicism as they were of my paganism. They envied my freedom. I envied them their confirmation. My friend Kevin explained to me the church's custom of "confirming" its members.

"You go to church and attend classes," he explained. "Then your uncles and aunts give you money."

From what he had said, confirmation was the church's chief rite of passage, recognizing those who came of age as its members. They marked the occasion with a celebration. Aunts and uncles came from all directions with cards of congratulation and monetary gifts. A child with enough relatives could clear several hundred dollars.

Envious of their good fortune, I asked my parents if I could convert to Roman Catholicism. They only laughed. "We're not Catholics," they said. When I asked them if we were Protestants, they laughed even harder.

"If by that you mean that we aren't Catholic," my father replied, "I guess you could say that. If a Protestant is a protest-ant, someone who protests against the church, then we are."

I had hoped he would say yes. I wanted to have an answer when people asked me about my religion. It embarrassed me not to know what to say. My family did not attend church, but at least I could say we were Protestants.

The first time I walked with my friends to St. Angela, they told me I could not enter. I was not surprised. I knew I was reprobate. Jerry, the older boy who lived next door, had said as much when I accidentally tore the religious medal from his neck during a tussle. "You're going to be damned for all eternity!" he thundered.

Certain he knew more about such matters than I did, I fled to my room for refuge. I threw myself down on the bed and sobbed, imagining the flames of hell licking at my feet for all eternity. I pleaded with God to forgive me, explaining I had not meant to break the medal. But like Esau, I felt I could find no place of repentance, though I sought it carefully with tears. So when my friends told me I couldn't follow them through the door of the church, I didn't argue. I knew my place.

As they disappeared inside, I peered through the glass at a statue of Christ mounted on a pedestal attached to the wall. His arms were spread in welcome, but not for me. Instead, he surveyed an empty hall below. There was a statue of Mary at the other end. She too had her arms spread, as if inviting an invisible audience to enter her embrace.

I gazed from one to the other for several minutes, my heart pounding. I was certain they might climb down and wave me away from the door at any moment. I wished I could step into the hall and examine the two figures more closely, but my friends were clear: I was not a Catholic. I could not cross the sacred threshold.

Being excluded from my friends' faith made it all the more attractive to me. I wondered what kind of strange rites went on inside that building. On Ash Wednesday they came out of the church with the sign of the cross on their foreheads, made from the ashes of the fronds they waved on Palm Sunday the previous year. I thought it gave them an air of macabre elegance. They gave up their favorite foods during Lent and went to the priests for confession. They lit candles. There was even a candle for the Holy Ghost. They said he was present as long as it stayed lit. Who knew where he went when the candle went out?

When the lesson ended, my friends appeared again in the deserted hallway, opened the door, and fled the place. The faint scent of holiness escaped with them, like the sweet and musty smell from an old woman's preserved wedding dress. I gave the statues one last nervous glance, just to make sure they had not sprung to life, and went off to play.

In my teen years I finally gathered the courage to enter the church. I visited at the urging of my sister's best friend. She was the first serious Catholic I had ever met and the first person to engage me in theological debate. She didn't want me to become a Catholic so much as to open my eyes to the reality of God's presence in the world. She saw him everywhere. He was infuriatingly remote to me, engaged in a cosmic game of hide-and-seek.

I visited the church on a Sunday morning, my heart skipping a beat as I passed through the door. I was afraid the priests might be able to tell I wasn't a Catholic, as if something in my demeanor betrayed the fact. I was aware there was bad blood between the Protestants and the Catholics. This undercurrent of tension gave an added thrill to my visit. I felt like a spy in the house of God.

I spent most of the morning trying to follow the order of service, a flurry of prayers, genuflections, and muttered hymns, interspersed with the priest's musical chanting. At one moment we were seated and then suddenly we were on our feet. When we weren't standing or sitting, we were kneeling. Uncertain about whether I was permitted to kneel as a non-Catholic but afraid that my failure to participate betrayed me, I sat on the edge of the pew hoping anyone who noticed would think I was *about* to kneel. I panicked when I saw people begin to exit the pews and make their way to the altar where the priest stood. Once in front of the altar, they opened their mouths and the priest placed something on their tongues. They bowed their heads pensively and knelt when they returned to their pews. I wasn't sure I should follow. But I worried that if I didn't, everyone would know I didn't belong. What would the priests do when they discovered a Protestant among them observing their secret rites?

As the worshipers at the end of my pew stepped out into the aisle, I made a bold decision. I decided the best strategy was to act like I belonged there. When my row began to move toward the altar, I followed suit and approached the priest. I was impressed by the way he served the congregation with machinelike precision. Worshipers came forward with hands folded and mouths open, like sparrows waiting to be fed by their mother. He muttered something unintelligible and placed a thin wafer on their tongues.

It may have been only my imagination, but the priest faltered slightly as I made eye contact with him. I was sure he saw through my ruse. Would he shout? Ask me to step out of line? I opened my mouth and felt the strange texture of the communion wafer, dry and tasteless, as it began to dissolve. Relieved the priest had not made a scene, I retreated down the aisle and took my place in the pew, trying to look both reverent and Catholic.

I left the church feeling exhilarated and considered returning the following Sunday, until I saw my neighbor's sister coming toward me with a frown. "I saw you this morning!" she said. It was an accusation not an observation. "What were you doing in our church? You're not a Catholic. Go to your own church next time." She knew as well as I did that my family did not attend church. I muttered something in halfhearted reply but did not go back.

Beulah Baptist was at the opposite end of Church Street. I was drawn there by a parade which took place at the time of year when summer stretches out like the rest of eternity. I was bored. None of my friends were around and I couldn't think of anything to do. Suddenly, I heard the sound of music and children's voices. Coming down the sidewalk was a makeshift parade of wagons, balloons, and someone dressed in a clown suit. A group of children marched behind waving. One of them ran over to me with a piece of paper inviting me to attend something called vacation Bible school.

This might be a good idea, though I felt some ambivalence about attending. The fact that I was unchurched didn't make me nervous. It was the "school" part that bothered me. I did not enjoy school. The thought of joining vacation and school together into some kind of hybrid was perverse, like the pictures one sees in the tabloids of babies reportedly born with the head of a dog and the body of a human. Who wants to go to school on their vacation?

Still, the clown was a hopeful sign. These people promised vacation Bible school was *fun*, an intriguing thought. I had never viewed church as a fun place. Perhaps the Baptist church was more like a circus—all colored lights and sounds and laughter.

Beulah Baptist, however, was all business. A large metal map of the world hung on the sanctuary wall just behind the pulpit, sprinkled with small pinpoints of light. I thought this was an odd choice for a decoration, more suited to the United Nations than a church. The map, I learned later, was meant to remind church members of the importance of missions. The people at Beulah were big on missions. Every day in vacation Bible school we were treated to a missionary story. I could never remember the names or the locations but the plot was always the same. Some child realizes the whole world is going to hell and dedicates himself to becoming a missionary. He leaves his weeping parents behind and goes to a distant jungle land. Communication with the natives is hard because he doesn't know the language. It doesn't help matters that the natives are cannibals. As he tries to tell them about Jesus, whose own story was almost as depressing as the missionary's, the natives capture him, cook him in a pot, and eat him. He is quickly replaced by another missionary who has been inspired by his sacrifice. The moral of the story, as far as I could tell, was, "Come to Jesus and this can happen to you too!"

I did not want to go to a distant country and tell cannibals about Jesus. I didn't even like being more than a block or two from my house. I certainly did not want to be boiled in a pot and eaten.

Beulah also had a weekly children's club, a combination of the Cub Scouts and vacation Bible school. Apparently these Baptists were good at creating hybrids. The gospel message, like the church itself, was presented each week in an unadorned, matter-of-fact way. Every Wednesday night we sat on metal folding chairs and listened as the leader described the torments of hell and the beauty of the cross. The message weighed heavily upon my soul. I knew I was a sinner and destined for hell. My Catholic neighbors told me as much. Now the Baptists said the same thing. My own conscience confirmed their accusation. Hadn't I once looked at a picture of Sophia Loren in a negligee? On another occasion, while whirling a jump rope over my head like a helicopter rotor, I struck a sparrow sitting on a fence and watched in horror as its small head sailed across the yard. The decapitated torso just stood there, frozen in place for a moment, and then the little body tumbled to the ground. For these and many other crimes I knew I deserved to go to hell.

By the end of the lesson I was sure everyone around me could hear my heart pounding. I could tell what was coming. The leader was about to ask us to "accept Jesus." He would ask us to lift our hands, "right where we were," and let him know we had prayed the sinner's prayer. I was too embarrassed to comply and too afraid not to. What if I was the only sinner in the group? How many sinners could there be in a room full of Baptists? But what if I didn't do it? The speaker said this might be my last opportunity. I might walk out the door, die on the spot, and be ushered into a Christless eternity that very night.

In the end, my fear of hell won out over my embarrassment. The metal folding chair groaned slightly as I lifted my hand. The leader asked us to repeat a prayer after him. It was as simple as that. Very neat and businesslike. A few days later I received a nice letter from the pastor of the church, a man I had never seen, congratulating me on my decision. I was proud of his letter, impressed by the way the pastor signed it in ink above his printed name. I read it over several times and then tucked it away somewhere in my dresser drawer.

Despite my pretensions to Protestantism, I felt as out of place at Beulah as I had at St. Angela. Most of the other kids who attended came for the game time. Apparently this was the fun they promised us when I attended vacation Bible school. But the only game anybody really wanted to play was dodgeball, and I was terrible at it. Overweight and slow on my feet, I was afraid of the ball. It was more like a half hour of target practice than a game, and it didn't take long for the predators in the group to spot the weak animal in the herd. I hated the way the leader's son called me by my last name instead of my first, uttering it in a way that made it sound like a character slur. I arrived every Wednesday with a sense of dread, embarrassed by my unfamiliarity with the Bible stories and afraid of becoming a target at game time. Eventually, I stopped attending.

Not everyone was unkind to me at the church. An older man named Joe took an interest in me. Unmarried and somewhat slow, Joe roomed at the YMCA. He phoned my house every week to check on my spiritual progress. Our conversations were awkward, confined to his labored observations about cold weather and long underwear. After a few weeks I asked him to stop calling.

Although I heard the gospel first at Beulah Baptist, I encountered Christ — really encountered him — in the back room of a Jack-in-the-Box restaurant. The fast-food joint was a mile from my home on a block that intersected Church Street coming from the other direction. Just graduated from high school, I was working the night shift, waiting on customers and cleaning the fryers. I am contemplative by nature, and the midnight shift only intensified my introspective tendencies. The situation in my family was an added burden. My mother was sick, wasting away from an illness that eventually took her life. My father's long-standing alcoholism grew worse. It did not help matters that my favorite radio station played only the blues after midnight. Before long I felt myself sliding into depression.

The thought of attempting suicide briefly crossed my mind, but only in the vague, romanticized way most adolescents consider it. The notion of actually taking my life made me feel queasy. If only I could handle the matter cleanly and in a way that insured I did not actually have to die. I considered inhaling gas from the jets beneath the grill, climbing underneath and taking deep gulping breaths near the burning flame. I fantasized about the grief those on the morning shift would feel when they found me slumped on the floor, just in time to save my life. But the only real danger I faced was of bumping my head in the narrow space. I eventually grew bored and gave up fantasizing.

It occurred to me that a spiritual focus might be the answer I sought. I dug out an old pack of Tarot cards hidden in my dresser drawer and tried to interpret my future from their obscure symbols. Inspired by George Harrison, I chanted "Hare Krishna" while scraping the grill, hoping it was the path to inner peace. It only made me dizzy. I prayed muttered prayers to the unknown God as I swept the floor, more petulant than penitent. Until finally, it occurred to me that the Bible was a spiritual book and I should probably read it. Someone gave me one when I attended Beulah Baptist. I dusted it off and brought it to work with me. During my breaks, I went into the back room and read the Gospels.

The Jesus I discovered wasn't anything like the one I had encountered during my pilgrimage up and down Church Street. He was not perched above the crowd gazing dispassionately at those below. I could easily imagine him walking into the restaurant and calling me to follow him. Nor was he the drab Messiah I had heard about at Beulah. He promised it would not be drudgery to follow him. "Come to me, all who are weary and heavy laden," he said, "and I will give you rest. Take my yoke upon you and learn from me, for I am gentle and humble in heart, and you will find rest for your souls. For my yoke is easy and my burden is light." I felt like heaving a sigh of relief as I read these words.

One night as I cleaned the restaurant and carried on a silent conversation with God, I complained. "If you're up there," I said, "I just want you to know I wish I had never been born!" I didn't really expect him to reply.

As soon as the thought formed in my mind, I noticed someone waiting at the drive-through window. As I came closer, I recognized him as a local "Jesus freak" named Dave. Dave provided the music and preaching at the Lost Coin, a coffeehouse sponsored by Glad Tidings Assembly of God, a Pentecostal church a few blocks from our house. I knew Dave from a distance. We had attended the same high school, where, like King Saul, he towered head and shoulders over the rest of the student body. I saw him during passing periods, his head bobbing above the sea of students like Jesus walking on the water.

Dave didn't say much as I waited on him. When I gave him his change, he grinned widely and handed me a piece of paper.

"If being born hasn't given you much satisfaction," it said, "try being born again."

I was stunned. I had not uttered my sentiment out loud, but someone had heard.

"Wow!" I said. "Thanks! Thanks a lot!"

Before long I started attending church again. This time it was at Glad Tidings, the Pentecostal church Dave attended. Glad Tidings met in a plain brick building that looked a lot like Beulah, only smaller. It had the same blond wood and bare walls, except for the baptistery, which had a picture of the River Jordan in the background.

The church's pastor, a bald man with thick hands and a round face who had once been a crane operator, turned red when he shouted from the pulpit. He clapped his hands and stomped his right foot in a Holy Ghost dance when he preached, as if keeping time to angelic music the rest of us could not hear. Every so often he cried, "Glory!" with a far-off gaze and the rumbling conviction of someone who could see something we could not.

The pastor reminisced about the old days, when the Spirit fell and God's people "got the victory." He began every prayer by say-ing, "Lord, we're a needy people." He intoned the words with such gravity we could not help but feel the crushing weight of the congregation's troubles bearing down upon us. It took our breath away. We reeled under the weight of it and clutched the pew. We had no idea! We *were* a needy people. God help us!

I had never witnessed anything like this. His preaching frightened and intrigued me at the same time. He whispered. During his message he displayed the entire range of human emotions. He shouted. He laughed. He wept. When he finished, I came to the altar and wept copiously, repenting of the same sins I repented over the previous week.

I have attended many other churches since then. I have been a church member and a pastor. Down through the years I have made a surprising discovery. Most of the Christians I know are disappointed with their church, finding it to be either too traditional or too modern. The sermon is too theological or not theological enough. The people too cold to one another or they are cliquish. In the end, the root problem is always the same. It is the people.

Yet Sunday after Sunday, these believers return to their pews, expecting God to meet them there once again. Some might view such attendance as an act of futility or as an exercise in wishful thinking. I believe it is a work of grace.

Eugene Peterson has written that when we get serious about the Christian life, we usually find ourselves among people we find incompatible. "That place and people," Peterson explains, "is often called a church. It's hard to get over the disappointment that God, having made an exception in my case, doesn't call nice people to repentance."

A few years ago I returned to the neighborhood where I grew up. I drove by St. Angela and saw the door through which my friends entered so many times to participate in the sacred mysteries of their faith. It looked like it needed a new coat of paint. I wanted to see if the statues of Jesus and Mary were still in their old places, dispassionately beckoning to the multitudes to enter their cold embrace. But I felt the old fear and did not get out of my car. I wondered if the smell of holiness still clung to the place.

When I drove by Beulah Baptist, I decided to stop in, thinking they might like to know how one of their prodigals had turned out. The pastor welcomed me with professional friendliness and listened politely as I told my story. A different man than the one who pastored the church when I visited on Wednesday nights in my youth, he looked tired. Distracted, perhaps, by the work he could have been doing if his time were not being taken up by this unexpected visitor. When we were finished, he thanked me for coming and retired to his study. I found my own way out.

The church where I worship today is neither mysterious nor drab. Its message is rooted in the hope of the cross and is consistently positive. Its decor is tasteful; its music terminally chipper. Yet I find there are times when I am filled with a quiet longing for the shadow of mystery and the unsettling scent of holiness. In many ways, I am still waiting for the Spirit to fall and for God's people to "get the victory." Wednesday night's children have all grown and gone, and the dodgeballs have long since been put away. Why, after all these years, do I still feel like a stranger in the house of God? I do not know. Nevertheless, I decided long ago to cast my lot with the church. It has probably failed me as many times as I have failed it, but I will not abandon it. I could not, without abandoning myself.

CHAPTER 2

Holy Days

On Halloween and Easter I ate candy. On Thanksgiving and Christmas I ate turkey and mince pie. Halloween was better than Easter and Christmas was better than Thanksgiving. Christmas was better than the first day of vacation. Better, even, than my birthday. Christmas was better than anything.

Easter, the most important day in the Christian calendar, was the least significant in my catalog of days. My Germanic ancestors celebrated it by recognizing the coming of the vernal equinox and by praying to their goddess Estre to make their fields and their wives fertile. Christians commemorated the resurrection of their savior on Easter by eating ham and chocolate. I had heard that the ham, my least favorite aspect of the holiday, was Christianity's way of thumbing its nose at Judaism. I didn't know who originated the idea of eating chocolate on Easter, but it was clearly the more sensible of the two customs.

Easter was marked by the visitation of the Easter Bunny, a minor member of the holiday pantheon, who supposedly appeared during the night and left candy for us children. This might have compelled me to rank this holiday higher on my list. However, exposure to our pet rabbit changed my view of the Easter Bunny. The rabbit was a gift from my father's best friend, who left it on our doorstep one Easter morning. We named the rabbit Sniffy, deceived by its cuddly appearance, and begged my father to let us keep it.

Sniffy viewed us with contempt and took every opportunity to bite the hand that fed him. He loathed human contact and on the few occasions we let him run free, scurried about leaving pelletlike droppings scattered throughout the house. This wasn't the sort of creature who hopped down the bunny trail "bringing every girl and boy a basket full of Easter joy." All of this resulted in a relationship of mutual aversion that compelled us to consign Sniffy to a wretched existence in our basement.

I did not think much about Christ on Easter. His most important day, as far as I could tell, was Good Friday. Good Friday was the day of his suffering and, since my mother refused to let me go out and play between noon and three o'clock on that day, of mine as well. These were the hours when Christ suffered, she explained. It was disrespectful to let me go out at that time. This scrupulous observance each year puzzled me. The rest of the year my mother regarded Christ with an attitude of polite neglect, even at Christmas. Why should she behave any differently on Good Friday? Her concern was not for Christ's feelings but those of our neighbors. She did not want them to think we were pagans. There was no choice but to comply with her wishes. So, on Good Friday, I remained indoors and tried to be appropriately grave as I contemplated Christ's suffering. At three o'clock, I put such thoughts aside and went out to play.

Easter's chief attraction for me was the basket I received each year. My parents filled it with eggs and bunnies made of chocolate, totems more befitting the Teutonic deity than the Christian God. They placed them on beds of artificial grass and surrounded them with a colorful assortment of jelly beans. The chocolate rarely lasted the morning, but the jelly beans, a candy of last resort, were often still waiting to be eaten when Halloween arrived. I saved them for desperate days when no other sweets were available. Like a squirrel who gathers nuts and then buries them for the winter, I always allowed a handful to settle to the bottom of the Easter basket and dug them out during the lean weeks leading up to Halloween.

Halloween was higher on my list than Easter. In the Christian tradition All Hallows' Eve was a time to commemorate the dead. The pagan Celts believed it was the night when the souls of the dead returned to visit the living. Although I was more attracted to the Celtic vision of Halloween than to the Christian, it was the quality of the candy that gave Halloween the advantage.

In our neighborhood, the observance of Halloween began the night before with something called Devil's Night. In later years Devil's Night evolved into something more sinister, a night when hooligans roamed the streets of Detroit setting fire to cars and abandoned buildings. But during my childhood, its rituals had more in common with the Lord of Merry Misrule in a medieval Christmas revel than the near riots that came in later years. We rang the neighbor's doorbell and then ducked into the bushes to hide so nobody was on the porch when the door was answered. We soaped windows and sometimes threw the occasional egg.

I considered Halloween to be autumn's last breath. The winter solstice was not due for several weeks, but I already felt its approach in the chilly night. On Halloween, my brother and sister and I donned costumes and went door to door with pillowcases in hand, begging for candy from the same neighbors whose windows we soaped the night before. Too excited to eat, we gathered in the living room at dinner, already dressed in our costumes, impatient to see the sun finish its slow arc into twilight. This was the rule, as every child knew. Begging could not begin until dark. We defined dark as the moment the sun dipped behind the roof peak of the house across the street or when the first cry of "trick or treat" was uttered by some child on our block, whichever came first.

The same unwritten code which decreed we must wait until dusk to beg also dictated that we wear a costume. Some were store bought, but mine were usually homemade. When I was younger the costume was as important as the candy. The costume had a power of its own. The cape or the mask transformed its wearer into an avatar. All the boys were heroes or villains. All the girls were enchanted and beautiful. It was easy to believe the spirits mingled among us. Halloween lost its mystery as I got older and my costume became a pragmatic necessity that merited minimal effort. A hobo was the obvious choice, requiring only an old shirt, a pair of my father's work pants, and the shadow of a beard, drawn with my mother's eyeliner pencil. By then, it was all about the candy.

I collected a vast assortment as I went up and down the block with my brother and my friends. A few parents shuttled their children from neighborhood to neighborhood in cars. My mother and father considered such parents crass opportunists, and although I publicly decried the practice, I secretly wished my parents did the same for me. A limitless supply was there simply for the asking for any who were enterprising enough to venture beyond the few blocks around our house. Who knows how many pillowcases I might be able to fill?

Chocolate, in all its various forms, was most prized. Hard candies and gum were valued least. Some items were treasured more for their uniqueness than their taste, like popcorn balls or the mini loaf of bread I once received. When someone handed out something particularly good, like the priests at St. Angela's rectory who gave out full-sized Hershey bars, word ran up and down the street like a fire, prompting us to try to visit the house more than once. This, of course, was also a violation of the Halloween code. Anyone who got caught could be sent from the door in shame without a treat.

At the end of the night I trudged home, weighed down and weary from carrying the load of candy I collected. Pouring it out on the living-room floor until it rose to a mountainous height, I sorted it by preference, carefully eyeing the growing piles forming in front of my brother and sister, anxious to see which of us had collected the most. I consumed the best of it in a matter of days, while the dregs might last until Christmas.

Technically speaking, my birthday was not a holiday, but it was sanctified by the giving of presents. We did not have parties. Mother permitted us to have only one, when we turned seven, but on our other birthdays we could have whatever we liked for dinner. I usually chose "swanky frankys," hot dogs wrapped in bacon and stuffed with cheese. There was always chocolate cake.

My birthday fell in August, far enough away from December to establish it in my mind as the coordinate pole opposite Christmas on the year's gift-giving axis. The birthday presents I received in August impelled my thoughts toward the gifts I expected to get in December and channeled my anticipation toward Christmas. In

December and January, I began to count the days until my birthday, brooding over the gifts I wished I had gotten at Christmas. The rhythm of my desires revolved around these two days, like a planet whose course is determined by the shared pull of two great suns.

I pitied those whose birthday fell in November or December. Most tragic of all were the souls unfortunate enough to be born on Christmas day. They were doomed to go through life suffering from a deficit of gifts, robbed each year of the additional presents which might have been theirs if their birth date fell earlier in the year. I wondered if it was possible to go to court to change one's birthday the way some people changed their name.

Compared with Easter, Halloween, and my birthday, Thanksgiving hardly deserved a place on the list of sacred days. It arrived without candy or gifts and with little in the way of vacation. The most it could boast of was a large turkey dinner, and it was the only other time in the year besides Christmas when I could expect to eat mince pie. Despite these limitations, this holiday actually surpassed Easter and Halloween in significance because of its proximity to Christmas. This was its charm. Thanksgiving was the harbinger of Christmas and marked the official start of the Yule season.

On Thanksgiving my mother, who usually slept until noon, rose early and put the turkey in the oven. She made dressing, stuffed celery with cheese, and baked two pies. I spent the morning checking her progress and stealing food from the relish tray. When the turkey was done, we moved the kitchen table into the "dining room," a space that served as the other half of our living room for the rest of the year, and ate. There was little else to set this day apart. There was nothing to do, since all of my friends were either away visiting their relatives, or entertaining them in their own homes. I ate, grew bored, and then ate again. In the evening, I calculated the number of days until Christmas and wondered if it would ever arrive.

I counted off the months, measuring my life holiday by holiday by this cycle of days like a traveler counting off the mile markers until he reaches his destination. The apex in this passage of days was reached at Christmas, the most important day of the year.

Although we possessed a manger scene, the tree was the true center of our Christmas celebration. Our Christmas ritual began with a pilgrimage, as we bundled everyone into my father's huge Chevy and drove the few blocks to a lot strung with colored lights. The pavement, covered with a light powder of snow, looked as if it had been dusted with diamonds and twinkled as merrily as stars. Overhead, a fuzzy speaker filled the night air with Christmas carols.

Evergreen trees lay on their sides in neat rows waiting to be inspected for purchase. We walked up and down picking up stray pine cones and spare branches in a vain search for the perfect Christmas tree. George and Lynn and I scattered among the rows and looked for likely prospects, propping up those that looked suitable.

"What about this one?" we asked, our eyes sparkling to match the glitter on the pavement below.

We circled any worthy tree like druids in worship, carefully examining it for flaws. But Father's determined refusal to begin the search before Christmas Eve meant the trees on the lot were already picked over. He claimed it was a matter of tradition, but we suspected it had more to do with the price. Our search was further complicated by differences in taste over the kind of tree we should bring home. I wanted a spruce, someone else wanted a fir. Grumbling about the cost of getting a real tree every year, Father said we should get one of those new artificial trees.

Our argument suddenly evaporated in a clamor of unanimous disapproval over this idea. My best friend owned an artificial tree. Its aluminum branches and tin foil "needles," illuminated by a tri-colored rotating disk, looked like something out of a science fiction movie. Father's threat galvanized us to action, prompting the selection of a battered Scotch pine with key branches missing. We stuffed the tree in the trunk of our car and made our way through the wet streets back home.

The real work began once we arrived at the house. We prepared our tree "stand," an old metal bucket which we kept in the basement primarily for this purpose. For some unexplained reason, my father preferred this to an actual tree stand. There was no way to secure the bucket to the base of the tree. We scoured the back yard and gathered an assortment of bricks, large stones, and small boulders to brace the tree so it stood upright. We brought them from the back yard in solemn procession, cradling our hands the way the Levites must have held the memorial stones they retrieved from the Jordan.

We spent the next hour working with the stones in the bucket, while someone rotated the tree in a futile attempt to get it to stand straight. Father looked on, barking directions mixed with expletives. It was his job to string the lights, retrieved from an old potato-chip can. Only then could we begin to hang the ornaments, each one carefully wrapped in tissue paper like a cherished family heirloom. We draped the branches with silver tinsel, flinging it by the handful onto the tree that towered over us. It fell around us in a glittering blizzard, landing in clumps on the tree and the floor. When we were finished, we stepped back to admire our handiwork, hands on our hips and breathless from the exertion, as my mother declared it the most beautiful Christmas tree she had ever seen. She said the same thing every year.

Occasionally, we awoke on Christmas morning to find the tree had toppled onto the living-room floor, either as a result of the stones shifting in the bottom of the bucket or because our cat had tried to climb it. Once, we found my father and the neighbor from across the street sprawled on the floor next to it. The jug of moonshine our neighbor brought with him to celebrate the holiday lay nearby.

I spent Christmas Eve playing beneath the tree, alternating between the small manger scene and a red Santa in a silver sleigh. Sometimes I combined the two, giving Santa a prominent place among the magi. I was intrigued by the story of the birth of the Christ child, my knowledge of it drawn largely from the few carols I knew and the pictures on the handful of Christmas cards we received. Arranging and rearranging the figurines, I examined their faces, as if hoping they might reveal the mystery behind their story.

I knew Jesus was the center of their tale; the star intrigued me even more. It appeared to announce the Savior's birth to the magi and guided them on their journey. I had seen pictures of the magi mounted on camels and profiled against the night sky, their gaze focused on the bright star that shown over the small village of Bethlehem. Sometimes I scanned the night sky myself, hoping the star would reappear and lead me too.

The pictures taught me that angels also played an important role in this story. One Christmas, I thought I heard angels singing outside my bedroom window. I climbed up and peered out into the darkness, the reflection of streetlights on a freshly fallen blanket of snow creating a supernatural light. When I opened the window, it grew louder. But it was only the sound of Christmas carols piped over a loudspeaker somewhere nearby. I shut the window, disappointed that there had been no heavenly visitation.

I even prayed to see an angel one night while lying in my bed. With my eyes squeezed tightly shut, I asked God to prove his existence by sending an angel. I mustered my energy and pleaded with all my might, hoping by strength of will to persuade him to show himself. After an eternity of waiting, I thought I sensed a presence at my bedside. My heart throbbed with expectation. It was true! God did exist. He had sent one of his angels to my room, just as he had to Mary and Joseph. I wanted to know what the angel looked like, but I was too afraid to open my eyes.

When I finally gathered the courage to open them just a crack, I could make out an eerie form in the shadows by my desk. This was too much. I put my hands over my eyes and told God I had changed my mind. I didn't want to see an angel after all. I peeked again after a few moments and saw, to my dismay, that the thing was still there. I prayed again and apologized to God for my brazen demand. I begged him to make it disappear, but something deep inside told me it was still there.

There was no escape. I must face the angel. No matter what the outcome, I gathered my courage and opened my eyes. The form was still where I had seen it. But this was no heavenly visitor, only a pile of dirty laundry. My angel turned out to be a trick played by the shadows that fell on the growing mound of clothes on the chair by my desk. God apparently did not dispatch his celestial messengers merely to satisfy the curiosity of small boys.

Santa Claus, on the other hand, left tangible evidence of his presence beneath the Christmas tree. The sudden and mysterious appearance of wrapped presents accounted for much of the thrill I felt on Christmas morning. It wasn't just the toys but the manner in which they arrived that intrigued me. Santa possessed supernatural powers. He had the ability to teleport and could read minds. He knew when I was sleeping. He knew when I was awake. He knew if I'd been bad or good. His nearest rival was God himself.

All this changed when my father accidentally revealed that he purchased the presents I found beneath the tree on Christmas morning. I was not entirely surprised by this news. I already knew there was no such thing as the tooth fairy. My ambivalence toward the tooth fairy had been growing for some time. When a tooth fell out, I placed it beneath my pillow and awoke in the morning to discover a dime in its place. I wondered whether it still counted if I chose not to wait for nature to loosen them and decided to pull several of my teeth for the cash. But it was the nearness of the tooth fairy that finally soured me on her. Santa and the Easter Bunny did their work at a distance. True, they had some uncanny way of getting into my house in the middle of the night, even when the doors were locked. But they did not come into my room. In fact, I had been assured that they did not want to be near me. If they caught me awake, they would leave.

The tooth fairy was different. She came right up next to my bed. She slipped her hand under my pillow. Moreover, she did it with such stealth, I was never aware of her presence. What if she appeared at my bedside one night with less benevolent intentions? I was terrified I might wake one night and find her looming over me. I began to fret. I worried so much, the next time I lost a tooth I worked myself into a state of hysteria and refused to go to bed.

"I don't want the tooth fairy to come into my room tonight," I said.

My parents tried to reassure me. They insisted the tooth fairy never harmed anyone, but how could they know for certain? All right then, they said, the tooth fairy wouldn't visit my room that night. But how could they make such a promise? The tooth fairy could pass through walls. Locked doors were no obstacle. She traveled where she pleased without a sound and no one could tell where she came from or where she went. Their efforts to comfort me only made me more alarmed. As a last resort, they reluctantly told me the truth. The tooth fairy was a myth.

Although I was momentarily relieved, this first crack in the foundation of my enchanted world undermined all I believed. Within a year all the old gods were dead, each one gone in quick succession. No tooth fairy. No Easter Bunny. And, of course, no Santa Claus.

The loss of Santa Claus hurt the most. It is hard to know why, since, outwardly, not much changed. We still put up a tree each year. The presents continued to appear under the tree on Christmas morning. But something had changed. This final blow left me feeling stranded in a cold universe bereft of magic and power. The knowledge that all the enchanted beings of my childhood were mere fantasies ultimately shook my belief in God himself. When my sister, Lynn, spoke to me of angels, I grew angry and cut her off.

"There's no such thing," I said.

"There is so," she insisted, upset by my challenge to her belief.

Feeling superior and cruel in my possession of the truth, I refused to relent.

"Naw, it's just like Santa Claus, the Easter Bunny, and the tooth fairy. Jesus and the angels are like that too. They don't exist. It's something grown-ups tell children." She went crying to my mother, who reassured her of things she herself did not believe.

Christmas changed again for me when I became a follower of Jesus Christ. I now understand and celebrate its true significance. Easter too has taken on new meaning. But I fear I have never quite recovered the sense of awe and wonder I once felt as a child. Perhaps that is why each year my Christmas tree is decorated with both angels and Santa Claus. I know it is why I return to the Bible again and again. God uses the truth of the Scriptures to reenchant my world. I turn my attention to its pages and discover a better vision of the world I lost, a place where heaven and earth meet and the sound I hear in the distance is once again a rumor of angels.

CHAPTER 3

The Haunting

Our house was haunted. Not by ghosts of departed souls but by my father's broken dreams. They were etched on the basement wall, where my father had sketched the life-sized image of a man's hand. The arm was outstretched, as if reaching for something just outside its grasp. Or was it extended in warning, a veiled threat to any who might venture near?

Either way, the image was a fitting icon for my father, who went to that dark corner of the house to wrestle with his dreams and lay them to rest. He piled them high, covering a large workbench shoved against the wall with mementos and unfinished projects.

An old ham radio was there, its voice silent and its Flash Gordon dials covered with dust. This hulking piece of equipment was a link to my father's army days. Drafted near the end of World War II, he went through basic training at Fort Hood, Texas. On the first day, he and all the other recruits were ushered into a large, graceless building where they were addressed by a grim master sergeant.

"Look to the man on your left!" the sergeant shouted.

Everyone looked to the left.

"Now look to the man on your right!" he barked.

All heads snapped to the right.

"Within a year, one of you will be dead!"

All the recruits were subjected to a series of exams and then slotted for various jobs. The woman who interpreted my father's battery of tests studied them thoughtfully. My father's scores were very high. Somewhere in the genius range. Then, with the gravity of a judge pronouncing sentence, she declared, "Young man, you owe a debt to society." This expectation annoyed my father. He did not want to owe anything to anybody. Besides, he was about to spend the next several years in service to his country and perhaps even give up his life. Didn't that count toward paying off whatever debt she supposed he owed by existing?

The army spared him the grim fate described in the sergeant's prophecy, due in part to his aptitude for electronics. The army shipped my father to the Antarctic, where he spent the last months of the war working with radios. He finished his tour of duty and returned to Detroit with a pair of snowshoes, a hand-carved walrus tusk, and a certificate to prove he had been at the bottom of the world. He picked up where he left off in an awkward relationship with his father—a medical doctor who practiced out of his home and a devout Roman Catholic who talked theology with the priests of his parish as he treated them.

I never met my grandfather, who died before I was born. My knowledge of him came through the stories my father occasionally told about him. The only photograph I have of him, taken in some long-forgotten summer, shows him towering over my grandmother. His basset hound face, framed by a pair of remarkably large ears, deep-set eyes, and a sharp chin, makes him look like someone who could as easily have been given to depression as to contemplation. My grandmother is on his arm, grinning at the camera. But my grandfather's smile looks more like a grimace, as if he has just chastened the photographer for some error.

He probably had. My father's stories about him depicted my grandfather as a meticulous man absorbed in his work and in his faith with little time left for his family. I could not tell whether my father admired him, but I knew the two did not have a warm relationship. Alternating between hot impatience and cool indifference, the resulting tension between them produced a swelling bitterness that grew like the painful boil that once formed on my father's neck when he was a boy. Mildly uncomfortable at its onset, the abscess eventually festered and grew hot. My father tried to ignore it, partly because he feared the treatment but more because he did not want to face the physician. His father, he was sure, would receive the news of this affliction as a personal affront. Eventually it grew so large and painful he could no longer hide it. My grandfather, now more doctor than father, took him into the office and lanced the boil in silent reproach. The poison drained and the pain went away. But my father's resentment needed a sharper instrument wielded by a more subtle hand.

Dad's aptitude for electronics prompted him to try to repair our broken television set, which sat on the workbench near the old ham radio. With its back broken open and its giant tubes exposed, it looked like the organs of some patient abandoned on the operating table. The set was a gift from my grandmother, purchased for us children so we could watch *Romper Room*. She felt the program had educational value but was most impressed by its moral message. This was evident in the "Do Bee Song," a bouncy ditty with a hypnotic refrain aimed at imprinting a primary code of ethics on our preschool minds:

> *I always do what's right,*
> *I never do anything wrong.*
> *I'm a Romper Room Do Bee,*
> *a Do Bee all day long.*
> *Do be a plate cleaner.*
> *Don't be a food fussy.*
> *Do be a car sitter.*
> *Don't be a car stander.*
> *Plate cleaner,*
> *car sitter,*
> *Do Bee all day long!*

The stark contrast reflected in the lyrics anticipated the moral struggle that followed us for the rest of our lives. I had not yet heard the apostle Paul's cry of anguish in Romans 7, "What a wretched man I am! Who will rescue me from this body of death!" I soon discovered Don't Bee was my alter ego, intent on deflecting "the good that we would do." I aspired to be a Do Bee in my mind but found I was a Don't Bee in my heart.

The show's live audience was made up of children who sang the songs and played the games as I watched. I wondered who they were and how they had been chosen to be on the program. At the close of each program, the show's host, Miss Flora, peered into a magic mirror, like some Delphic priestess exercising the gift of second sight, and named those who were watching at home.

"I see Billie and Suzie and Jimmy," she chanted.

I listened intently, anxious to hear my name called but certain it would not be. I listened anyway, each time with renewed hope and heart-pounding fear. To hear my own name would not only prove the efficacy of the magic mirror, it would give me a place among the elect. It would mean I was like the children I saw on TV and was within reach of their enchanted world. Just as the dead strain to hear their names when they are read from the great book on the day of judgment, I longed to hear Miss Flora declare mine. My heart sank each time it was not mentioned. To be unnamed was to be unknown. I wondered why I was out of sight, beyond the reach of the mirror's magic.

I have often experienced this mixture of hope and despair — every time I have waited for my number to be called in the raffle or watched in vain for my name to be posted among those who have made the cut. The same longing compelled me to press in at the edge of the lunch table where the cool kids sat in junior high school, desperately hoping someone from the inner circle would speak to me and grant me permission to move to a higher place. I squeezed into the waiting crowd dressed in paisley and imitation suede only to find I was invisible to them. I lacked the appropriate marks of grace. My hair was too curly, my waist too thick and short. I did not live on the right block. I did not have the right friends. Like Lazarus at the gate or Dives in hell, I was permitted to watch from a distance, but I could not enter that particular paradise.

This is familiar territory for all who dwell on the outskirts of desire. It is the realm where dreams become narrowed, shaped more by the certainty of exclusion than by the hope of fulfillment. For my father, its boundaries were marked by the old pallette daubed with paint that lay on the workbench near our broken television. The paint was shriveled and dry but a faint scent of oil still lingered.

A large easel stood next to the workbench. This was no amateur's toy but a great bulky thing with a blank canvas mounted on it. The canvas, prepared by my father for painting, waited in vain for his hand to bring it to life. Some exigency of daily living compelled him to set it aside and he never went back to it. In the background, etched on the basement wall in a kind of ironic counterpoint, was the hand my father had drawn, as if it were Adam half formed, still stirring in the dust and waiting for his creator to get around to finishing the task.

Standing in the darkened basement, I imagined the hand belonged to a being from a dimension that existed beyond the wall. I suspected it possessed the ability to pass through at will. Sometimes I stood in the shadows and stared at it without blinking, hoping to see it step fully into my realm of existence. The unfinished form and the blank canvas were emblems of the great disappointment in my father's life. The former was a specter of his unfulfilled dream of becoming an artist. The latter served as a silent reproach, there to remind him of his failure to follow through on this goal.

My father attended art school after his time in the service and studied with a man who had written a book about drawing. He was not a great light in the art world but a minor star in that constellation. Relics of that period in my father's history were scattered throughout the house. A yellowed still life hung on the kitchen wall depicting a table with some fruit on it. It looked like something a beatnik might have hung in his apartment.

A watercolor showing an alley in Detroit hung in the hallway off our living room. A solitary figure stood in the smoky glow of a single street lamp, and behind him the dark houses lay in shadow. I was sure the image was a self-portrait and that the painting depicted the narrow streets of my father's childhood. Eventually, I came to understand that all my father's paintings were self-portraits. Some were overt, like the stern profile depicting him as a young artist, sharp jawed and unsmiling, tucked away in one of our closets. Others were implicit, like the painting which showed Christ's descent from the cross. A figure my father later identified as himself stood on a ladder braced against the cross removing the Savior's scarred body. Was this an act of devotion? Or did he see himself as one of the pagan soldiers, merely doing his duty? The figure was too enigmatic to tell.

The painting that disturbed me the most showed a bearded Abraham with his son Isaac bound on the altar. Abraham's knife is raised high, caught in the terrible moment between the command to kill and the order not to strike. I had never heard the story of Abraham, and what little my father could tell me of it made no sense. Had God really told Abraham to kill his son? Why utter such a command? If God had done so, why did Abraham obey? Most disturbing of all, what would my father have done if he were told to do such a thing?

I don't recall my father telling me the rest of Abraham's story. Perhaps he had not read it. Years later I read it for myself and learned of God's command to withhold the knife and of his provision of a substitute. But in those days all I knew was what I could see: a son bound and passive and a father dispassionately determined to kill. I never asked my father who he identified with in the picture, but I think I know. The cold hand that held the knife was the same one that put the lance to his neck. It was my father who lay on the altar, waiting quietly for the blow to fall and the blood to flow.

My father's favorite piece hung in a place of honor in the living room. It was tall and narrow, done in the abstract style in gray and gold and textured by mixing sawdust and paint.

"What is that?" I asked when I first saw it.

"Can't you tell?" he answered with a grin. "It should be obvious."

I examined the painting to see if I could identify some familiarity in its strange image. Was it a person or an object? Something about the painting reminded me of the hieroglyphics drawn on the walls of an Egyptian tomb. It might have been the image of one of the gods of the ancient world, a man with a bird's head, both familiar and alien at the same time.

I studied the painting many times as if it were the Rosetta stone, able to unlock the secrets to my father's soul. I thought I detected something that might have been a monk's cowl and a pilgrim's staff, but I could not be sure. The images disappeared as soon as they took shape. One moment I saw the figure of a man traveling along a path. I looked again and it was an apparition emerging from the mist. I searched for clues in every hue and stroke but felt no more enlightened when I finished than when I began. The meaning of the figure in the painting, a mirror of my father's true self, was shrouded.

My father was still a student when he and my mother married. She supported them both at first, working at an airline ticket counter. But when she became pregnant with their first child, the doctor took my father aside.

"You had better go out and find yourself a job," the doctor declared.

My father found work at an automobile plant the next day. The job's greatest challenge was its monotony.

"I spent eight hours a day, sitting in a chair and watching the parts as they came off the assembly line," he told me. "Eventually, I could read a novel and do my job at the same time."

He hated it.

After my brother, George, was born my mother did not go back to work for the airline and my father did not return to art school. I was born a year and a half later, and my sister, Lynn, followed in quick succession. My parents moved from their tiny apartment in the city of Detroit to the blue-collar suburb of Roseville, Michigan. They parked our bulky Packard in the drive, planted a spare lawn soon overrun by crabgrass, and settled in to wait for the American dream to arrive.

Every morning before the sun came up, my father put on his white shirt and left my mother sleeping in her bed to go to work at the automobile factory. In the evening, as the sun slipped behind the trees on the other side of the street, he returned home again to find her seated on the living-room couch, brandishing a lit cigarette with the languid serenity of Hepburn or Garbo. They ate dinner and watched television.

On weekends, Dad spent the day drinking vodka and listening to old jazz records. Occasionally he played along on his cornet, trying unsuccessfully to match the skill of his idol, Bix Beiderbecke. The music depressed me, its toddling melody a mirror of my father's drunken gait as he stumbled down the hall into bed at the end of the night. My mother usually did not follow him. She stayed up into the early hours of the morning smoking Lucky Strikes and brooding, the glowing ember of her cigarette floating in the dark like some wayward star without a constellation. On many nights the two fought and on some they made love, the sound of their love barely distinguishable to my ear from the sound of their violence.

My father approached suburban living with a casual disinterest that disturbed our neighbors. They kept their lawns with an almost compulsive tidiness, while ours grew long and wild. Dandelions flourished on our lawn until their bright yellow heads turned grey and exploded in a shower of seeds that scattered throughout the surrounding yards. When one of us poked a hole in the screen door, my father replaced it with a large piece of plywood. A cracked basement window went unrepaired for decades, and the address by our front door hung sideways, a fitting emblem for a home where everything was slightly askew.

I attributed this state of general disrepair to my father's bohemian values. What else could be expected of an artist? He could not be bothered with things as mundane as house repair or lawn care. Such pursuits were for those who lacked artistic vision. I was proud of our untamed lawn and saw it as an emblem of our libertarianism. We did not go to church. We did not celebrate Easter. We did not weed our lawn.

Following his example, I too disdained yard work. I drew on the basement wall, adding my own stick figures to the image in the corner. I found a leather-bound sketchbook filled with drawings and cartoons my father made while a student in art school. I pored over the pages and tried to imagine the stories behind the characters. Eventually I took up a pen and tried to mimic the strokes. Sketching my copies next to his, I tried to match the originals so precisely that others would think they were my father's.

When I showed them to my father and told him I hoped to become an artist someday, he was displeased.

"Don't bother," he said. "You should become a plumber instead. They make more money."

But I took my father's example to heart. He chose the path more traveled and found it a disappointment. If I understood his mistake, perhaps there was hope I might travel a different path. I wondered if the secret was to keep my dreams spare. If I narrowed my choices to one, would I be more likely to see my dream realized? Or perhaps the key was a matter of focus. If I ran toward my goal and didn't allow myself to become distracted from it, I might avoid the stumbling block that kept my father from reaching his dream. The key, I thought, was to discover the one insurmountable obstacle that stood between my father and his dream. If I could avoid it, then I might succeed where he failed. Gathering my courage, I asked him what kept him from becoming the commercial artist he always wanted to be. He looked at me for a silent moment. Then his eyes narrowed as the corner of his mouth turned up in a bitter and crooked smile.

"You did," he said. "You kids did."

I don't remember feeling hurt or angered by his remark at the time. I merely accepted it as a fact and wondered how his life might have been different if we had never been born. This, at last, was the cipher to his soul. Here was the secret sorrow that haunted him. Those things others might have viewed as the trappings of success, he considered to be marks of failure. We were a living and daily reminder of the dream that eluded him. This explained the undercurrent of resentment I sensed when he stepped into his role as father.

In time my father painted over the basement walls, along with the pictures I had drawn. All part of an uncharacteristic flurry of home improvement, he dug up the front lawn, leveled the ground, and planted new grass seed. He laid white tile on the grey cement floor and hung wood paneling to finish off the basement. But he did not finish it all. Instead, my father walled off a portion, creating a kind of inner sanctum, and left that part of the basement just as it was.

Most visitors to our home were not permitted to cross that threshold. The few who did saw my father's workbench covered with mementos from the past and remnants of projects he never intended to finish. There was the old ham radio still collecting dust and the collection of vacuum tubes from the television set he once tried to repair. There was the palette daubed with colors, still waiting for the touch of an artist's brush, while nearby the large easel, with its mounted canvas still blank, leaned against the workbench like a siege engine drawn up against the bulwark of some ancient fortress.

These items were piled high, like wood upon the altar. While in the shadows just beyond, a faded image on the wall stood sentinel over them. My father's drawing of a man's hand remained there until the day he died, its ghostly arm outstretched. As if grasping for something just out of reach.

CHAPTER 4

If Wishes Were Horses

"I wish I had a new bike," I said.

"If wishes were horses, beggars would ride," my mother replied.

This obscure saying was my mother's conversational doomsday machine, capable of shutting down any complaint. She repeated the last phrase for effect, or perhaps just to annoy me, which was the more certain outcome.

"What's that supposed to mean?" I asked.

She merely smiled sagely and shook her head, as if to say she felt sorry for the person who failed to grasp something so obvious.

Years later I learned the verse was an old English proverb that eventually became part of a Mother Goose rhyme:

If wishes were horses,
beggars would ride.
If turnips were watches,
I would wear one by my side.
And if "ifs" and "ands"
were pots and pans,
there'd be no work for tinkers!

Mother was a small woman weighing barely a hundred pounds. A dark-haired beauty in her teens, she posed for a photograph that once hung in the Royal Museum in Regina, Saskatchewan. A copy of the picture also hung in our living room. She posed for it holding an apple with a bite taken out of it, her coquettish grin belying the life of hardship she endured during her childhood.

Born Phyllis Townsend, she grew up during the Great Depression, the youngest child of Catherine Rita Doyle and John Beecher Townsend. Catherine Rita Doyle was a woman of thoroughly Victorian sensibilities who listened reverently to the queen's Thanksgiving address every year and lectured teenagers on the evils of spitting. She was a member of the United Church of Canada and wrote uplifting quotes by Henry Ward Beecher and Edward Bulwer Lytton in the flyleaf of her Bible.

John Beecher Townsend was something of a rogue, even though his middle name paid homage to a distant family tie to the pious Bostonian preacher Lyman Beecher. If this was meant to inspire my grandfather to follow in his ancestor's godly footsteps, it proved to be a miscalculation. Piety was not John Townsend's strong suit. A smart dresser with a taste for liquor and a penchant for gambling, he once owned a chain of movie theaters. One of them, Mother claimed, was kitty-corner to the famous Grauman's Chinese Theater in Hollywood. This was destined to be my grandfather's lot in life—always just a few steps short of fame and success. After the stock market crash of '29, my grandfather moved his family to the Canadian prairie and started over. He opened a photographic studio in Regina and then opened another larger studio a few years later. But he drank and gambled away his profits, letting his family go hungry.

Grandfather disappeared for months at a time, leaving my mother's older brother, Jack, to support the family by selling newspapers. Money was so scarce it was not unusual for them to go for days without eating and to share a single can of beans at some meals. When my grandfather reappeared, unannounced and without explanation, after one of his jaunts, my uncle Jack threw him out of the house and told him not to come back.

"I watched my brother kick him down the stairs," my mother told me.

Grandfather got a job for a short time at the General Motors plant, after they reopened it to make munitions for the war effort, and then he disappeared for good. Mother never saw or heard from him again. She didn't know when he died or where he was buried. She kept a picture of her father from a more prosperous time, wearing a derby and a diamond stickpin, along with a few artifacts from his studio, in her hope chest for the rest of her days. It was the only legacy he left her. Except for his roguishness; she inherited that as well.

Mother was inclined to trouble in her youth. In the class designed to teach Canadian girls how to become proper young women, she took a dish towel and did the Dance of the Seven Veils when her teacher left the room. When the teacher returned to the room unexpectedly while Mother was in midstep, she let the towel fly, anxious to distance herself from the evidence of this unladylike conduct. It sailed through the air and landed on top of a freshly baked lemon pie. She escaped punishment when the teacher mistook it for meringue topping because of her poor eyesight. On another occasion, she sneaked out of school by crawling on her hands and knees so the teacher wouldn't see her. Once outside, she ran off to "meet the boys."

The place my mother felt happiest was on the stage. Regina had an active theater program, and my mother performed in several productions. She caught the attention of someone in the Canadian Broadcasting Company who encouraged her to enter the theater as a career and offered her a job performing in radio dramas. Uncertain of what to do, she turned to my grandfather for counsel.

He was quick to answer. "Don't do it," he warned. "In the end they will break your heart." This was not what she hoped to hear, but she took his advice

"It was the only advice he ever gave me," she explained. "I felt I had to take it."

She claimed not to regret her decision, but I was not convinced. Like my father, she too was haunted by the specter of what might have been. At times she tried to impart her knowledge of the theater to us, assigning us parts and staging dramatic readings at home.

Mother dropped out of high school at seventeen and came to Detroit with only five dollars in her pocket. She found lodging at a girls' club in the city and proceeded to steal boyfriends away from the other residents. One Valentine's Day, she received five boxes of chocolate, all from different suitors. Mother attracted plenty of admirers in her day, beginning in grade school when one of the boys in her class wrote to express his love for her saying, "You have a big nose."

She was sometimes pursued by strangers. A friend once handed her an expensive pair of nylon stockings, saying it was a gift from an acquaintance who wanted to take her out on a date. Suspicious, my mother asked her friend who the man was and what he did for a living. The woman said he was involved with the union and his name was Jimmy Hoffa. She declined the invitation.

Mother dated a general who hinted the government knew Pearl Harbor was about to be bombed before the attack and a toy inventor who bought a new suit and forgot to remove the tags. Another date took her to an amusement park, where she rode a roller coaster for the first time and was so terrified by the experience she tried to jump out of the car in the middle of the ride. She had to be restrained by her date. When the ride ended, my mother promptly bought another ticket and rode it again alone, just to prove she could do it.

Mother fell in love with a soldier who died in the war, then fell in love with another who broke her heart. Eventually she met my father's best friend, a charmer with an Irish tenor who introduced them after he lost interest in my mother. My father told me he fell in love with my mother at first sight, but my mother was not especially interested. She, however, told the story differently.

"The moment I saw your father," she said, "I knew I would marry him. I felt like I had come home."

They believed they were lovers in another life.

While single, my mother supported herself by selling tickets for a major airline. One of her regular customers, an elderly gentleman from a nearby mental hospital, visited her each day and asked for a ticket to Mars. She made out a "ticket" and sent him happily on his way. During the lunch hour, my mother went down the street to

Hudson's department store and spent it riding the escalators. They didn't have anything comparable in Regina.

In those days the airline allowed its employees to fly free when there was an open seat on a flight. She flew to some of the cities she always dreamed of visiting as a girl, but couldn't afford to stay the night. Instead, she turned around and came back on the return flight.

"At least I could say I had been there," she explained.

Mother's traveling days ended when she got married. My father didn't like to travel and rarely went farther than our back yard on his vacations. The only flight I ever knew Mother to make after she married my father was a trip to New York when her sister Marge died suddenly. I considered Aunt Marge to be our most glamorous relative. She qualified for this title on several counts. First, she lived in New York. I knew from the old movies my mother watched that it was a place of tall buildings and nightclubs. She was also a writer. Before moving to New York she worked for the *Windsor Star*, writing their society column. When my aunt first applied for the job, the editor simply laughed. He told her he didn't hire women to be reporters. The next day she came back and applied again. The answer was the same. She returned the next day and told the editor that she planned to keep coming back until he hired her. The editor gave her the job.

Aunt Marge's divorce only added to her mystique, as far as I was concerned. Mother was tight-lipped about the circumstances. We knew she was once married to a photographer who worked for the paper. Mother claimed he was handsome but hinted at some dark secret that led to the separation. I thought Aunt Marge's divorce gave her an air of intrigue and sophistication like Elizabeth Taylor.

Mother learned about Marge's death over the phone. She claimed she knew someone was dead the moment it rang. Grandmother was on the other line, frantic because Aunt Marge hadn't answered her phone for several days. The police broke into my aunt's apartment and found her lying like Elvis on the floor, the victim of a heart attack. Mother traveled alone to New York to attend the funeral. She was pensive when she returned and talked about her sister. When they were small, the two of them used to catch bed bugs and race them at night. When she was a girl Aunt Marge had naturally curly hair that she wore in ringlets. Mother was always a little jealous of her sister, convinced that her mother considered Marge the prettier of the two girls.

With three small children to care for and no driver's license, Mother was housebound except for the occasional trip to the hairdresser or the shopping center a mile or two from our house. For those trips she usually took a cab. This had not always been the case. Mother did have a driver's license for a brief period. She claimed she passed the driving test by playing on the examiner's sympathies. I was sick and in the hospital at the time. She wept and said that without a license she would not be able to visit. She claimed the examiner passed her, even though she flunked the driving test.

On one of her first excursions the car stalled out a few feet from our house. She sat in the middle of the road for several minutes until a passing driver offered to push it to the side. He got behind the vehicle and gave a mighty heave, but without effect. He tried again with the same result. Finally, he came around to the side of the car and asked my mother to roll down the window.

Exasperated, he pleaded, "Lady, will you please take your foot off the brake."

Eventually Mother decided the roads were safer without her and let her license lapse. She tried driving again in the late '60s when she felt housebound and trapped. This time she asked my father to teach her to drive. My brother and sister and I watched from the front window as she steered our blue behemoth of steel a few short feet down the driveway into the street. It took about an hour. The plan was to drive to the corner, turn right, and then circumnavigate the block. It was simple enough. But once the car was in the street, Mother panicked. She gripped the steering wheel the way a drowning person clutches a life preserver and jammed her foot on the brake, desperately afraid the car might actually move. The vehicle sat there, immobile, for at least a half hour as my father urged her with increasing aggravation to give it some gas. When he began to lose patience, she stamped on the accelerator, only to panic again and slam down on the brake as she felt the car lurch forward. For the next hour my father's Chevy inched its way down the street, staggering forward in fits of acceleration and then coming to a sudden stop, as if the driver couldn't decide whether to proceed. At last it came to a halt three houses away at the stop sign on the corner.

By now Father was ready to call it quits, but progress emboldened Mother. Instead of making the right, she decided to turn left, ignoring his plea to stop. She turned the car with easy grace, right into oncoming traffic. My father, his face flushed red from shouting moments ago, now went pale with fear and gaped at the driver in the approaching vehicle. Mother, however, was unfazed.

"Why doesn't that fool get out of the way?" she demanded.

Father was silent, too paralyzed to point out that she was driving on the wrong side of the road. He gripped the armrest as beads of sweat appeared on his forehead and waited for the inevitable collision. At the last minute, my mother swerved to the right side of the road and pulled to the curb. She and my father exchanged places and he drove the car home. She never attempted to drive again.

My father blamed his aversion to travel on his military days.

"I traveled enough in the army," he said. "I don't want to go anywhere."

The closest my parents ever came to taking a family vacation were our occasional day trips to Monroe to see relatives. To me, going to Monroe meant going to the "country." To get there we drove south on the highway until the neat rows of suburban tract homes gave way to farmers' fields dotted by red barns emblazoned with Mail Pouch Tobacco signs. The roads changed from pale white to dark chocolate and melted under the heat of the summer sun. The sweet scent of oil radiated from the road in waves of shimmering heat, like incense rising from the altar. After what seemed like a lifetime, the painted profile of two Indian chiefs came into view, the signs that marked the entrance to the street where my favorite uncle lived.

My parents always said we were only visiting for the afternoon, but we knew we would end up staying late into the night. At midnight, after making the rounds of our uncles and aunts, we drove to Stony Point and rolled up to a tavern my parents frequented during their courtship. My brother and sister and I ordered colas and drank them in glasses, hoping the adults around us believed they were mixed drinks. We begged for change to put in the jukebox and danced to Dean Martin and Perry Como. We peered through the darkness of the room, watching the lovers at the other tables watching us and trying to ignore my mother's tears.

Something about these visits always made my mother cry. They ignited some spark of longing for the past within her. Or was it regret that enveloped her in that place, bitter as the grey cigarette smoke that filled the room and made our eyes smart? Once, when we pulled out of the parking lot to start our long drive home, my mother jumped out and ran off into the night. My father swore, jammed on the brakes, and went after her. We tumbled out of the car and followed him in the darkness, uncertain whether we should laugh or be afraid. For all we knew, this might be some grown-up version of tag or hide-and-seek, except for the tremor of fear and hint of anger we heard in my father's voice as he called her name.

My father vanished in the shadows, and we stumbled after him, out onto the beach where the black expanse of the lake intersected with the night sky to form a wide horizon. In the distance, where the darkness spilled over the edge of the earth, I saw the lights of some slow-moving freighter wink on and off. We found Mother sitting on a rock in the moonlight, watching the tide and sobbing. When I asked her why she was so sad, she said the lake was the only place she knew that made her feel like she was back on the prairie. It lay bare the longing in her heart, bringing its wreckage to the surface the way the tide stirs the depths and scatters its debris along the shore. She bore little resemblance to the laughing socialite I imagined from the stories of her past. What, I wondered, had transformed her into this sad woman who wept on the beach and spent her nights at home brooding in the dark?

The older I grew, the more I suspected Mother of carrying some secret she could not divulge. I could sense it whenever we talked about her past, a familiar spirit darting about the edges of her conversation. It appeared suddenly, like a face hidden in the shadows, and then just as quickly drew back without warning.

It took form one cold spring when my mother announced she was going to have a visitor. This was itself a rare occasion. Although Mother had a few friends, she spent most of her days alone, limited by her inability to drive. This mysterious visitor, we were told, was a woman named Millie and her daughter. We knew very little about Millie, only that she lived in California and had been my mother's best friend many years ago. Mother kept a gold locket in her dresser with the inscription "I will remember Millie" engraved on it.

Even more curious was the fact that the three of us children were not permitted to witness the meeting. When Millie and her daughter arrived, my mother sent us out of the house. Millie's daughter had raven hair and green Irish eyes. My brother, George, later remarked that she looked more like our mother than her own. She entered the house with Millie, while we stood on the front lawn, grumbling about being excluded from such a significant event and wondering what they might be talking about. After about an hour the visitors stepped out onto the porch and said their goodbyes. We waved as they climbed into a waiting car and drove off. I never saw them again.

Back in the house my mother looked troubled, as if she might have been crying. The three of us peppered her with questions, but her answers were vague and unsatisfying. We pleaded with her to tell us what the visit was about, and she finally said that Millie came seeking advice.

"She thinks she's having a nervous breakdown," Mother said. "She wants to end her life."

"What did you tell her?" we asked, wondering what counsel she could have given powerful enough to stay the hand of someone bent on such a terrible design.

"I told her, 'You can't. You have a child to think about,'" she explained.

"Did she believe you?" I asked, wondering if a simple statement was enough to change the will of someone bent on their own destruction.

"She had no other choice," Mother replied.

Years later, when we learned about Mother's secret, my brother conjectured that Millie's daughter was actually our half sister. By then it was too late to find out the truth. What was clear was that my mother's spirit eventually buckled under the weight of her secret sorrow, whatever its source. It bore down so hard she took a razor and slashed her wrist in the middle of the night. I heard her cry, coming long and low from behind the bathroom door, like an animal caught in a painful trap who knows it cannot escape. Standing in the hall, my father rattled the doorknob and repeatedly begged her to open, unable to repress the grim panic in his voice.

I pulled the sheet over my head and plugged my ears, praying to God to make it stop. As if in answer, her wail of despair was suddenly cut off, the ensuing silence more terrifying than the commotion that preceded it. In desperation my father kicked the door in and lifted her crumpled form from the bathroom floor and carried her to the bed.

Neither said anything to us the next day about the incident or about the bandages on my mother's wrist. I asked her what had happened, already knowing the answer.

"I cut myself opening a can," she said.

Despite the counsel she gave to her friend Millie, Mother tried to take her own life two more times. Her body eventually achieved for itself what she failed to accomplish by her own hand. Her health began to decline the year after I graduated from high school. At first we thought it was a common case of the flu, until she took to her bed for several weeks. The doctors were mystified by her condition and the treatments they prescribed only made her feel worse. My mother, who spent so much time wishing she were dead, suddenly found the will to live. But by then her body refused to cooperate. Whether from the ravages of hunger she suffered in her childhood during the Great Depression, or as a result of the emotional depression she battled for so long during adulthood, her body just gave up. Mother never came home from the hospital.

"If wishes were horses," my mother would say, "beggars would ride, beggars would ride." When this conversational doomsday machine failed to silence our complaining, she used another that annoyed me almost as much. "Be careful what you wish for," she said, "you just might get it." It might have been her epitaph.

CHAPTER 5

Shadow of a Doubt

Sunday was the worst day of the week. At least as far as television was concerned. On Sunday mornings the cartoons I enjoyed on Saturdays were replaced by religious programming. There was *Davey and Goliath,* an animated cartoon featuring a boy and his dog whose adventures inevitably proved the point of some biblical story I had not read. I watched weekly, captivated by the Gumby-like quality of the animation while vaguely uncomfortable with the moral of the story.

There was also a program called *Mass for Shut-Ins.* The ministrations of the priest were intriguing, but I was disturbed by the thought of what it meant to be "shut-in." I pictured adults sent to their rooms and held there against their will, with windows closed and doors locked.

My favorite program featured the filmed tent crusades of a prominent faith healer. Each week I watched with morbid fascination as a menagerie of the ill and infirm gathered around him in the hope of being blessed by his healing touch. The evangelist asked each to tell his or her story before laying hands on them. Their litanies of misfortune had a familiar ring, sounding like the contestants on *Queen for a Day,* who competed against one another with their hard-luck stories. The winner, chosen by audience applause, was awarded fabulous prizes.

The television evangelist operated on the same principle. Once the tale of woe was told, the evangelist took the sufferer by the hand. He spoke with authority, but not to God. Instead, he addressed the afflicted.

"Be healed!" he demanded.

This was not a request. He may as well have been daring the poor soul not to be healed.

"Go ahead!" he seemed to say. "Make me a liar! I dare you."

Who could refuse?

On other occasions he addressed the affliction, like an angry parent calling for an errant child who fled to the closet to hide.

"Arthritis," he cried, "come out."

The command to be healed was always accompanied by a touch. Sometimes it looked more like a slap. The evangelist placed the heel of his hand on the suppliant's forehead and gave it a light bop. Knees buckled as the afflicted went down, with shouts of "hallelujah" all around. Those who failed to fall with the first touch were blessed with a second. If the first touch didn't do the job, the second always did.

"Be heeealed," he declared, drawing out the vowel. "In the name of Jeeesus!"

I suspected the miracles were staged. But the evangelist always interviewed the sufferer afterward, offering irrefutable evidence to skeptics like me.

"How does that arm feel now, sister?" he asked. His smile showed us he already knew the answer.

"Praise the Lord, it feels fine."

"Praise the Lord!" he agreed.

Just in case her words of testimony weren't proof enough, he asked the healed for a demonstration of their newfound health. They flexed their arms, hopped on lame feet, and threw away their crutches.

Occasionally he appealed to those of us watching at home to bring our needs to him by touching the television screen. I reached out my hand, nervously scanning the room just to make certain there was no one else to see, and placed it on the spot he indicated. Was it the power of God I felt or only the crackle of static electricity? I wasn't sure.

Absence from church did not keep me from praying. I may have been godless, but I was not entirely prayerless. I called on God whenever I felt the need for immediate and divine deliverance. Like the morning I spilled the gallon jug of milk. Horrified as the cascade of white liquid spread across the kitchen floor, I asked God to let me get it cleaned up before anyone discovered what I had done.

"If you let me clean this up without anyone finding out, God," I pleaded, "I will never sin again."

I did not keep my promise.

In those days my theology of prayer was shaped by a child's experience of living under powers and principalities who, in their own godlike way, did as they pleased without explaining their reasons.

My prayers felt like the petitions I sometimes made to my parents. The greater the request, the more ambiguous the response.

"Mom, can I get a new bike?"

"Mmm, we'll see."

This was not quite a no, which was encouraging, but neither was it a yes.

Such an answer occupied that mysterious no-man's-land between wish and fulfillment children know so well. This is a region where the atmosphere is a mixture of hope and disappointment — only as much hope as is needed to keep our wildest dreams at bay, and not enough disappointment to kill them altogether. My prayers vanished like a child's wish, quickly uttered and soon forgotten. The result was anyone's guess.

This made what I saw on Sunday mornings all the more intriguing. The evangelist not only claimed to have the healing touch, where God was concerned, he had the power of command. He called and God answered. The reply was immediate. The proof, as far as I could tell, was tangible.

Since then I have come across many who claim the power of God is in our hands. The key that unlocks it, they say, is faith. In the early days of my Christian experience, I attended church with Pentecostals who were convinced God was enthroned in heaven just waiting for a chance to break out in our midst. All he needed from us was a little faith.

But that was also the catch. God's power, like a raging fire, was more than able to engulf any problem I might set it against. I, however, had to provide the kindling. That power, I was told, was also a deep well supplied by a limitless spring. But like any well, the pump needed to be primed. Great answers to great prayers did not take much faith. They required only as much faith as the grain of a mustard seed. God might as well have asked for a silo full. Don't get me wrong. I could pray my way into the occasional parking space. But when it came to greater matters, my faith was smaller than a mustard seed.

My deficiency of faith became painfully evident a few months after I graduated from high school when illness descended upon my mother. I began attending the Lost Coin, a coffeehouse sponsored by Glad Tidings, the Pentecostal church a few blocks from my home. Flulike at its inception, my mother's illness lingered for weeks. We thought nothing of it, expecting her to be up and around in a matter of days. We let the dishes pile up in the sink. A mountain of laundry began to build beneath the clothes chute. My father suggested she go to the doctor, but she refused. (He would have done the same had their positions been reversed.) All she needed was a little rest, she said. She would be fine in no time.

When my mother began to dehydrate, my father took matters into his own hands. He picked her up and carried her to the car—she was too weak to walk—then drove her to the doctor. The doctor prescribed some pills and sent her home. She still couldn't keep anything down, not even the medicine that was supposed to make her better. Eventually they admitted her to the hospital. This, we were all sure, was only a temporary measure. Mom had been hospitalized before. She would be home in a few days. We ran out of clean dishes and began to take our clothes from the dirty pile.

While in the hospital, my mother asked me to pray for her. I had told her before the illness of my decision to become a follower of Christ. Nervous about how she might take the news, I waited for an opportune moment. It came one afternoon while she cooked dinner.

"Hey, Mom. Guess what?" I said, as she watched something simmer on the stove.

"What?" she asked.

"I've decided to become a Jesus freak."

Without missing a beat she replied, "Oh, that's nice honey."

Then after a pause, she added, "I think."

Over the next few months we discussed my commitment to Christ. She was happy for me but nervous. She worried that the church would let me down in the end and that the disappointment would be too much for me. She was uncomfortable with some of the things I said about Jesus' being the only way to God.

"I've known some bad people in my life," she said, "but I don't know anybody who is bad enough to go to hell."

I wasn't sure how to answer her objection. I didn't know much theology. Only that we were all sinners and that Christ died to pay for my sin.

"People who claim to be Christians are some of the meanest people I know," she added.

I couldn't disagree. I searched for an analogy to help me make my point. "Mom," I finally said, "in the pig sty every dirty pig looks clean." I'm not sure she understood my point.

Now that she was in the hospital and still not improving, she wanted me to intercede with God on her behalf. She was having trouble keeping her food down and the doctor said she could not go home until she could eat. Dangerously thin, she still had no appetite.

"Pray that God would help me to eat," she pleaded with tears in her eyes. Then she asked me to finish her Jell-O, to make the doctor think her appetite had returned. To encourage her, I gave her a card with two verses from Psalm 139 printed on it: "If I take the wings of the morning, and dwell in the uttermost parts of the sea; even there shall thy hand lead me, and thy right hand shall hold me."

And, of course, I began to pray for her. But the more I prayed, the worse she grew. She still could not eat. She grew weaker, not stronger. We finally started cleaning the house and doing the wash.

Meanwhile, I tried to bolster my faith by reading verses about prayer. Jesus commended those who possessed great faith and admonished those who doubted. Ironically, those who spent the most time with him usually exhibited the least amount of faith. My friends at the coffeehouse were convinced the secret to success was to act as if God answered your prayer despite what your eyes might tell you. Someone suffering from a bad head cold told me God had healed him. He sneezed as he said this and blew his nose. "It may still look like I have a cold," he explained, "but praise God, I've claimed my healing and I'm not going to let appearances deceive me."

This sounded more like wishful thinking than faith to me. But perhaps he was right. Maybe God was merely waiting for me to act. What my mother needed was a prayer with authority. Like the televangelist I watched as a child, I decided to "claim" a healing for her.

By now she was no longer conscious. She looked fragile lying in the hospital bed, as if she might shatter when I touched her. She stirred gently as I gingerly took her by the hand. It was bruised where a needle pierced the vein.

I began to whisper.

"In the name of Jesus," I prayed, "be healed."

She sighed but did not awaken. I could see no visible improvement, but I tried not to think about it. I was determined to act in faith and not let my eyes deceive me or rob me of God's answer.

"I claim your healing, in Jesus' name."

Asleep in my own bed a few days later, I woke with a sudden start at 2:00 a.m. The house was eerily silent and the air tinged with expectation. Something was about to happen. But what? I started to pray and was startled again when the phone rang. It was the hospital. My mother was dead.

I never saw my mother's face again. My grieving father could not bear to have an open casket at the funeral. I understood his reasons but wondered whether it was a mistake. Not because an open casket helped us move through the grieving process quicker but because it might give God one more chance to perform a miracle. What, I wondered, if God's plan all along was to raise her from the dead? What better way to bring my father to the point of faith? Secretly, however, I was relieved. I did not want to see her shrunken by death. Most of all, I did not want to touch her body now that its soul had fled. In order for God to raise her from the dead, I might need to lay hands upon her.

You might think God's failure to answer my prayer would lead to a spiritual crisis. It was, after all, the great disappointment my mother had feared I would one day face. I was a little surprised myself that I did not feel bitter about the outcome. But everywhere I turned I saw tokens of God's presence in my life.

One evidence was God's orchestration of my mother's funeral. Since we had no church of our own, my father left it up to the funeral home to choose the minister. They selected a Baptist minister who chose Proverbs 31 as his text and spoke of the blessedness of the godly woman. I could not help laughing at the choice. My mother was no Baptist. She was a chain-smoker who liked her beer, gave birth to a child out of wedlock, and used language no Proverbs 31 woman said.

Most of all, I was encouraged by what appeared to have been a movement toward faith during the last days of my mother's life. We spoke about God. She asked me to pray. Her last words to me were, "I'm trying to believe the way you believe." Best of all, the minister preached the gospel at her funeral. I could not have arranged it better if I had planned it myself. Still, I could not help smiling at the unintentional irony of it all.

I have prayed many other prayers since that day in the hospital. Sometimes I get the answer I want. Often, I don't. I ask anyway.

The Prodigal

My grandfather was a doctor. When his patients couldn't afford the hospital, he performed the operation on the kitchen table while my uncles administered the anesthetic. He was a devout Catholic who treated the priests and nuns of Sacred Heart parish in Detroit and liked to talk theology. He gave money to the church and sent his children to a parochial school. My dad rejected his faith. He considered the church hypocritical and spent most of his life running hard in the other direction. Like the prodigal in Jesus' parable, who set out for a far country, Dad began to chart a course that took him as far away from his parents' values as he could possibly get.

Things came to a head between them shortly after my father returned home from the service. My grandparents were troubled by the lifestyle they saw their son living. They didn't approve of the people he associated with or the way he spent his time. One morning as my father shaved, my grandfather walked into the bathroom, pointed an accusing finger at him, and declared, "Bill, I've got my eye on you." My father glared back at the image in the mirror and snarled, "You know what, Dad? You're just a little too late."

When my father turned his back on his parents' religion, he turned, instead, to a personal blend of Eastern mysticism and the occult, with snatches of Buddhism thrown in for good measure. It was a personalized religion without a name. There were no formal rites of worship and no churches. He was both its high priest and sole adherent. Its major tenet was the belief that life continues after death.

My father was obsessed with the supernatural. He was particularly interested in stories about ghosts and reincarnation. He read all the writings of Edgar Cayce, "the sleeping prophet," who claimed to have been a reincarnation of Jesus Christ. He subscribed to *Fate* magazine, a publication that regularly featured stories about UFOs and ghosts. He believed he and my mother had been lovers during a previous life. He believed that more than anything else.

The passion that convinced my parents they were lovers in a former life sometimes burned with a different kind of heat. They fought late at night after the children went to bed. My mother hurled a shot glass at my father with such force it left a dent in our front door. My father threatened to burn down the house with a kerosene lantern. When morning came Dad got up and went to his job as if nothing had happened. I learned to dread the long nights when I cowered in my bed and listened in secret as they brandished their disappointment like a blunt weapon.

During my teen years our relationship grew more troubled. The normal tension of adolescence was further aggravated by my father's drinking. The alcohol made him irrational at times and even cruel. When his best friend committed suicide, he disappeared into his bedroom to weep in private. After he emerged, he glared at me. He swore and said, "You should have been the one to die."

"Bill!" my mother gasped. "He doesn't mean it," she explained, trying to shield me from the verbal blow. I just shook my head. I wasn't about to let on that his words hurt me. I wondered if it was only the vodka talking or if they expressed his true feelings.

At the peak of our conflict, he walked into the bathroom one morning while I shaved and glared at me with disapproval. "I've got my eye on you," he said.

"Guess what, Dad," I shot back, "you're just a little too late!"

His eyes grew wide with recognition, and then with a sad laugh, he said, "That's just what I said to my father. I was shaving when it happened too." He walked out of the room shaking his head at the irony.

My father was angry when my mother died. He was angry with the doctors who were unable to treat her problem and angry with my mother for leaving him behind. Most of all, he was angry at the inequity of a world where such things could happen to two lovers. "I was faithful to your mother all through our marriage. I never went out on her once, and look at what I get for it," he complained.

I was angry too, frustrated over the chaos that now reigned in our house. As my father's alcoholism grew worse, he no longer confined himself to binge drinking on the weekend. Now he was drunk most nights of the week. He disappeared for days, staying overnight with the women he met in bars or at singles' clubs. Sometimes he was too tired to report for work. He drank so much he woke up drunk and started the new day with a shot of vodka. The smell of it, like sour cologne, emanated from his pores.

Our house, never a tidy place prior to my mother's death, soon became layered with clutter. Beds went unmade for months on end. Floors went unwashed. We selected our clothes each morning the way the Israelites gathered manna, picking the day's wardrobe up from the floor where we'd dumped it after removing it from the dryer.

Always impatient with the normal upkeep that comes with owning a home, my father's strategy for handling problems alternated between the extremes of outright neglect and bizarre attempts to fix what needed repair. When our toilet began to back up, he ignored it for months. Finally, he decided to remedy the situation with a bottle of hydrochloric acid. This might have been a good plan if only he had warned me before I used it. The burning sensation let me know something was wrong but didn't leave any permanent scars.

All the while, he bore his grief like an open wound. Sometimes he tried to comfort himself by taking out the box from the dresser drawer where my mother's ashes were stored. He cremated her according to her wishes but could not bring himself to inter the remains. The one-sided conversations he held with them were as heartbreaking as they were hilarious. Usually he berated her for dying and leaving him behind. She, of course, responded with silence, a technique he used on her many times during their arguments while she was alive. I do not know whether she was able to take any pleasure from such revenge.

He also took comfort in pouring out his heart to me. He spoke for hours about his loss and sorrow. He complained about the unfairness of it all. He spoke of the love he felt for my mother. When I saw him in the naked light of his grief, I discovered an unexpected pity for him. To my dismay, I realized he was not so different from me. Like me, he was hurt, confused, and uncertain of the future. There was a time when I felt I could bring my broken world to him, confident in his ability to fix it. Now his world was in ruins, a world shattered by a blow so great, no human hand could piece it back together again.

We traded roles. I cooked dinner, replaced the garbage grinder, and repaired the toilet. I worried about him when he didn't come home and sometimes worried even more when he did. One morning I went into his bedroom and found a rifle beside his bed. I was surprised he hadn't considered using it sooner.

Because I was now a Christian, I began to talk to my father about Jesus. He became angry at first. One evening, noticing that I prayed silently before dinner, he told me to pray out loud for everyone. Suspicious of his motive, I declined, but he continued to insist.

"Thank you, Lord, for this meal . . ." I began.

He interrupted.

"What do you mean, 'Thank you, Lord'? How about 'Thank you, Dad'? My money paid for the food. I cooked it for you. You're living under my roof and wearing clothes I bought for you. Don't give me this 'Thank you, Lord' crap!" I went back to praying silently.

On another occasion he listened intently as I explained the gospel to him. When I was finished there was a glint of understanding in his eyes.

"Are you telling me that when Jesus Christ died on the cross, he paid for my sins?" he asked.

"That's right."

"Every sin I have ever committed?"

"That's what the Bible says."

"So if I put my faith in him, I will go to heaven?"

"Yes."

I began to pray. This was the most receptive my father had ever been. Could this be the reason God allowed my mother to die? Perhaps it was the leverage my father needed to bring him to his knees. I hardly dared to breathe as I waited while he reflected on the things I said. After a long pause, he exploded.

"That's not fair!" he shouted. "I don't want Jesus to pay for my sins. If anyone is going to pay for my sins, I'll pay for them myself!"

He threw the Bible across the room.

My father eventually remarried. While his sorrow abated somewhat, it never really disappeared. It was always in the background, like a lingering ache from an old wound. For years I was afraid he might turn to suicide for relief, and in a way he did.

Fourteen years after my mother's death, I stood by my father's bedside and watched helplessly as he suffered from the consequences of a lifetime of alcohol abuse. A weary-eyed doctor told us nothing more could be done for him. It was only a matter of time before he died. As his biological systems shut down one by one, I listened to the whir and click of the machines beside his bed, uncertain of what they were supposed to monitor and wondering what their mysterious numbers revealed about the collapse taking place inside him. He seemed frail and helpless. Surely this broken man was not the same one who carried me on his shoulders when I was a boy. Could this be the man who one July fourth marched around the entire block, blowing "The Stars and Stripes" on his trumpet, while his children tumbled after him in merry procession?

I thought of the weekend I moved out of the house without warning. I was angry because he wanted to start charging rent. My father went away on a trip. When he came home, I was gone. I think he was hurt, but we never spoke of it.

I thought of the day my wife, Jane, and I moved across the country to attend seminary. We said our goodbyes on his porch. He wished me well and gave me a hug, but it was the look in his eyes that haunted me. I recognized the pain reflected there. It was the same expression I saw when he spoke of my mother.

I thought of my son, only a few months old, and realized there was a time my father held me in his arms with the same joy I felt for my own son. It was there, despite the reservoir of hurt I still carried with me, that I made an amazing discovery. I realized I loved my father.

I do not think this was what the psychologists call denial. Nor do I think this love was the result of suppressing my true feelings. I still feel the sting of my father's abuse and do not excuse it. But I have come to terms with the anger I felt over his alcoholism. These things did not stop me from loving my father then, and they do not keep me from loving him now that he is gone. It is the nature of children to love their parents and to expect to be loved in return.

Parental love, when it is healthy, is the same. I do not love my children because they try to do what pleases me. Their obedience is important to me; I expect it. But I loved them long before they were able to do anything in response to my command, and if they break my heart in the future, I know I will love them still.

It was this I discovered at my father's bedside. Not just my love for him but ultimately God's love for me. His love is the prototype of all human love. In some small measure it is reflected even in love that has been distorted by human sinfulness. God's love does not fade with time or disappointment. It cannot be broken by the ravages of sin.

As I stood at my father's side, I tried to carry on a conversation. "Dad," I whispered, "is there anything you want to say?"

"No," he gasped. He was in too much pain to talk.

I blinked back the tears and whispered the only thing I could think of to say. "I love you, Dad."

Instantly, as if it were a reflex, he whispered back the phrase I heard come from his lips so many times as a child.

"I love you too, Johnny."

They were his last words to me.

CHAPTER 7

Leaving Paradise

When we saw the tree, my best friend, Larry, and I decided to claim it. Located on a large tract of undeveloped land that lay behind the row of houses just across the street, it made us feel like we'd landed in paradise. A crumbling sidewalk ran through the field's center, the forgotten remnant of some politician's master plan. The landscape was covered with weeds and tall grass and was dotted with a few stunted trees. My favorite was a gnarled apple, ancient and twisted like an old man's fingers. It bent so low it might have been trying to claw its way free from that spot and move to some more verdant location.

But like most explorers, we soon found others were there before us. Someone had hammered three pieces of wood into the trunk. The makeshift ladder led to the remains of a weathered platform. There was no sign of its builders.

The discovery was unsettling at first. I worried those who constructed the platform might suddenly appear and accuse us of encroaching on their property. But I climbed the splintered rungs anyway and perched on one of the old tree's branches. The sticky afternoon heat, swollen with the buzz of insects and the sharp smell of wildflowers and weeds, lulled me into a trance. Larry and I would build a tree house on the old platform, move to the field, and live off the land like Daniel Boone and Davy Crockett. I would spend the night there. I would bring a girl here and kiss her on the lips in the milky light of the full moon.

But we did none of these things. After a few days Larry and I abandoned the tree, forsaking its branches for a hole in the ground. This decision was sparked by my unexpected acquisition of a genuine, military-issue entrenching tool. The small implement was less than half the size of a regular garden shovel with a head that could be folded and used like a pick. Larry and I carried it with us during one of our forays into the field and decided to try it out near the base of the tree. After a few shovelfuls of dirt, we decided to dig a proper hole. The ease with which we accomplished this inspired us to attempt something greater. We determined to embark on a project befitting our status as adventurers, something so grand we were sure no one had ever attempted it before. We planned to dig the deepest hole in the world.

We threw ourselves into the project with the kind of obsession that comes naturally to children at play, shoveling all through the afternoon and into the early evening. When the sun sank below the rooftops and the porch lights started to wink on, we finally headed home, our faces flushed from exhaustion and our hands rubbed raw from the wood of the shovel. The next morning we came back and started again. We were pleased when the hole was knee deep and marveled when we realized it reached our waist. Every milestone spurred us on to greater effort, until at last we declared the great excavation complete.

This was not a hole one could step into. To reach its depths you sat on the edge and dangled your legs over the side. Perhaps it was not the deepest hole in the world, but it was the largest I had ever dug. I fancied it was deep enough to trap a lion, or at least a large dog. We found a piece of plywood lying nearby and covered it with dirt and grass. When we squatted low and pulled it over our heads, it made the perfect hiding place.

The two of us spent the afternoon in the dark seclusion of our new fortress, watching spiders crawl up and down its dirt wall and planning to pass the entire summer there. But the next morning Larry decided we should fill the hole. He was afraid that someone might walk through the field at night, not see our handiwork, and fall in. To me, this was the chief beauty of what we accomplished. Our fort doubled as a secret hiding place and a trap for the unsuspecting.

I argued strenuously for leaving the hiding place intact, but Larry's conscience wouldn't let him. We spent the rest of the morning filling the hole with dirt and rocks. When it was high enough that someone who stumbled into it wouldn't fall too far, we abandoned our work and went to the small mom-and-pop store at the edge of the field.

The little store was the chief center of commerce in our neighborhood. My father referred to it as "the great facility." He got the idea from the owner, a big man named John, who proudly declared, "I am providing a great facility for the community." The comment struck my father as funny. Whenever he left for the store he said, "I'm going to the great facility to get some cigarettes." We just called it the little store.

We children were drawn to the place, like the moths that darted and spun in the lamplight of its parking lot at night. Captivated by the penny candy that lined the counter, we congregated there the way biblical women gathered at the well. A nickel was enough to purchase a whole fistful of candy for its owner. A dime bought a day's worth and a quarter was pure affluence. I dreamed of becoming an adult someday and spending an entire dollar on candy at the store.

Soda pop was another important staple we procured in our visits there. I liked a chalky brown liquid that looked like chocolate milk but tasted like soda. There were shelves of cupcakes, fruit pies, and pastries. One of my favorites was a frosted confection that purported to be Cuban Spice Cake. It wasn't the taste that attracted me so much as the exotic promise of its label, which made me think of palm trees and sandy beaches. It was probably made in New Jersey or Ohio. After the Cuban missile crisis, the unfriendly political climate forced the manufacturer to change the name to Hawaiian Spice Cake. The new name somehow made the treat less appealing to me and I switched to Coconut Cream Pie.

In that Promised Land of childhood delights, the entire wall behind the counter was devoted to candy bars. Favorites didn't mean much with so many possibilities to choose from. Deciding was an agony of delight. I stood at the counter clutching my coins in sweaty palms and deliberating over the vast selection. Sometimes I spread my money out on the counter in front of me and queried the owner about the possible combinations.

"What can I get for this?" I asked.

Whatever the suggestion, I inevitably pressed him further.

"Can I get anything else?"

I rarely accepted his first suggestion, eager to hear every possible combination. Once the list was exhausted, along with the owner's patience, I reluctantly made my decision, handing him my damp money and leaving with the goods. The pleasure I took from my purchases never quite measured up to the anticipation I felt when I entered the store. I always left feeling a measure of remorse, reflecting on the things I might have purchased with my coins but didn't.

On muggy summer nights a huddle of teenaged boys, their dark hair slicked back and a pack of cigarettes rolled into the sleeves of their white T-shirts, lounged in front of the store. They slouched against the wall, striking that delicate balance between childish nonchalance and adolescent menace. Smoking and occasionally spitting into the gravel at their feet, they eyed the customers who passed by, ever alert for anyone who might be sympathetic enough to buy them some beer.

When asked, most customers merely grunted a refusal and hurried past. But occasionally a passerby responded with a furtive glance and a knowing chuckle. A few minutes later the boys could be seen walking up the gravel road with beer in hand, trailed by a sleepy-eyed debutante with a beehive hairdo and a nervous giggle. Intent on finding their own kind of paradise, they disappeared into the field, leaving empty bottles strewn about like fruit fallen from the trees and scattering shards of broken glass along the old sidewalk.

I went to the field less frequently as I got older, eventually using the broken sidewalk only as a shortcut. On those occasions, I always looked for the old tree, its drooping branches bowed at the trunk like a fighter in defeat, and next to it the old pit with jagged rocks still protruding. Something about the sight always stirred me to sadness, the soul's melancholy sigh over a childhood passing too fast. I could feel adulthood bearing down on me and with it the cares that come with being worldly wise. The field shrank and its beauty faded as I grew and the glory I once saw in it disappeared. In the end it was only a field spotted with scrub and brush and a scattering of shriveled trees. The Eden I once knew was hidden from my sight.

Paradise took a different form during my senior year of high school, when I stayed for a time on Decker's Mountain with my high school friends. Jack, Gary, Ray, and I traveled there the day after graduation, rolling through Michigan and Ohio until we reached the green hills of Pennsylvania, where Ray's grandfather owned a cabin. We were determined to get back to nature, on the road like Jack Kerouac and loaded down with enough brown rice to last the entire summer. Gary, hook nosed and cadaver thin, was devoted to brown rice the way some people are devoted to religion. He assured us it was all we needed for the summer. Gary planned to go to college at summer's end to study Japanese and perfect his macrobiotic lifestyle, combining Asian philosophy and health food. As far as I could tell, it meant living mostly on brown rice and sea salt. The rest of us didn't know what we were going to do yet. I thought I might become a poet but wasn't sure how one entered such a career.

The cabin was surrounded by trees and lay at the end of a one-lane road that wound about halfway up the mountain. A few feet away a small brook bubbled through a rock bed where tiny lizards sunned themselves. There was no plumbing or electricity. We planned to get our heat from the wood-burning stove in the living room. But when we cleared out the cobwebs and tried to light it, we discovered a nest in the smokestack. The cabin filled with smoke and the four of us stumbled out onto the porch choking and laughing.

I spent the first night unable to sleep, unnerved by the complete darkness. I had never been in a place without some kind of artificial light. I lay in the bed and held my hand close enough to my face to feel my breath. But the form was invisible. The darkness was so thick a flick of my wrist might have sent it swirling in waves about my head.

Wrapped in shadow, I lay in the old bed waiting for dawn and listening to the unfamiliar sounds of the mountain. A night bird called from the woods and the brook chuckled in soft reply. Somewhere in the old house a board creaked as something scampered across the roof. Overhead, far above the tree line, the unseen stars moved in their courses and wheeled silently above the face of the turning earth. At last, I passed into a dream, surrendering to sleep the way a body on the threshold of death relinquishes its hold on life and gives up the ghost.

When I was a child I willed myself to stay awake at night, afraid my soul might forsake its body during slumber and leave me hollow. I did not want to become an empty shell. My father's parents both died in their sleep. And so, I was certain, would I. Or worse, I feared sleep might give way to a death that left me a prisoner in my body. Unable to speak or move, I would no longer be alive but still be conscious of the fact I was dead.

Sometimes I imagined my funeral and subsequent burial, haunted by the thought of being encased in wood and interred forever in cold earth. I determined never to close my eyes, only to awaken in the morning light to find, despite my vigilance, sleep had once again carried me to its domain. I felt robbed whenever sleep, silent as death and often as sudden, crept up on me at night. But that night on Decker's Mountain, disturbed by the strangeness of the place and my invisibility in the absolute dark, I welcomed sleep.

The next day I awoke cold and sore and realized with dismay that my morning routine now involved a trip to the old wooden outhouse behind the cabin. The prospect held a certain romantic charm for me when we first planned the trip. Now I realized the romance was really just ignorance. I had never seen an outhouse before, except in cartoons, let alone used one. I glanced nervously at the hole in the roof and then into the pit, wondering in succession about the relative danger of wasps and snakes.

Breakfast, like dinner the night before, lunch later that day, and dinner again in the evening, consisted of brown rice served with stale macrobiotic bread. I spent the morning browsing the few books that lay tumbled against an old bookshelf. Most of the titles and authors were unfamiliar. Their covers were weathered by age, and humidity had wilted the pages. I finally decided on an ancient volume of *The Jungle Book* by Rudyard Kipling and settled down on the couch.

I hadn't been reading long when I realized someone outside the cabin was shouting. I went out on the porch to see Ray down by the brook, running in circles as he brandished a homemade spear in one hand and a lizard in the other. He made guttural noises. Jack was doubled over, laughing hysterically. Then Jack took off his shirt and began to follow Ray. Gary sat on the porch observing the scene with a bemused look.

The mist that hung low to the ground in the morning was burned off by now, its chill replaced by the steam of midday. Jack took a large rock from the stream and laid it on the ground. Shouting something about needing to appease the gods, the two of them placed the lizard on the slab, doused it with lighter fluid, and set it on fire.

The whole thing was meant to be a lark, but I thought I could discern a disturbing sincerity in their actions. Watching the smoke and flame rise from their altar, I thought of William Golding's thesis that the veneer of civilization is only as thin as the social pressure placed upon us to maintain it. Perhaps, like the schoolboys in *Lord of the Flies*, we all would revert to a primitive state by the end of our time on the mountain. Later I tried to explain my reservations to Jack, but he laughed it off and said I was making too much of the incident. He and Ray meant nothing by it. I shouldn't take it so seriously. They were just having fun. That night we dined on brown rice and stale bread again.

The next day I walked down to the brook to look at the place where they immolated the lizard. I found the stone slab next to

the brook and on it the burned carcass, as if it were still waiting to be claimed by some deity. I saw a black spot on the rock
where the flash of fire scorched it. Was this a sign of what we were
becoming?

I came to the mountain with the intention of staying the entire
summer. The breaking point in my resolve came when we decided
to go into town to Ray's grandparent's house. The visit reminded
us of all the things we were missing. They had a washing machine
and a dryer. There was a fully appointed bathroom with a shower.
These amenities were attractive enough. But the real challenge to
my aspiration to "get back to the garden" came on the trip back up
the mountain.

Like pilgrims who have set out for the celestial city but must
travel through Vanity Fair, the road back to the cabin ran past a
Kentucky Fried Chicken. Amazingly, it was Gary who suggested
we turn in there. Gary was the one who first suggested we live on
a diet of brown rice all summer, assuring us of its power to purge
our system of impurities. If by that he meant the mere thought of
another mouthful of brown rice would make me gag, then it was
working.

But Gary did not need to work hard to persuade us to backslide.
We tumbled out of the car with an urgency that was hard to rec-
oncile with our commitment to dietary purity and descended upon
the little stand with a fervor one does not usually associate with
fried chicken.

Once inside, we might just as well have stumbled upon a working still somewhere on the mountain. The sight of so much fried
chicken, all golden brown and bathed in the warm glow of the
heat lamp, had the same effect on our self-control. Any thought of
dietary purity we might have harbored vanished as we succumbed
to the spell of hot grease and the Colonel's secret recipe. Our col-
lective willpower collapsed and we embarked on a binge of buying,
emerging from the restaurant with several buckets of fried chicken,
a mountain of macaroni salad, and a large bag of potato chips.

We did not have brown rice for dinner that night.

I awoke the next day feeling much the way Adam and Eve must have felt the morning after they took the fruit from the serpent. My innocence shattered and my resolve broken, I knew I could not stay on the mountain much longer. This might be Eden. My friends certainly thought so. But I was unfit for such a place. The comforts of civilization were too important to me. I wanted to live in a house with electricity and a bathroom. I wanted a furnace to warm me when it got chilly at night. I wanted to watch television. I did not want to eat another meal of brown rice.

I picked a dead moth out of the bucket of leftover chicken and munched on a leg, wondering absently whether our lack of a refrigerator made a difference in the flavor. I counted the number of pieces left over and tried to calculate how many meals it might provide. I doubted it would last until noon. The chicken was already starting to go bad. That meant brown rice for lunch and dinner again. My stomach turned over, either from the unrefrigerated chicken or the thought of eating more brown rice. Perhaps it was both. I knew I couldn't last the summer.

I left Decker's Mountain a few days later, two months and three weeks short of my goal of staying the summer. Gary was my ticket out. In fact, he was the first to announce he couldn't stay the entire time, but for a different reason than mine. The diet and the outhouse did not bother him. He wanted to go home to get a summer job so he could pay for college in the fall. Jack and Ray were incensed. They felt we had betrayed the plan. Gary's leaving complicated matters for the two of them, because he was the only one with a car. Despite this, Jack and Ray announced their determination to stay. They planned to remain on the mountain for the rest of the summer and then hitchhike home in the fall.

Gary and I packed our things and left. Watching the cabin recede in the distance, I felt a mixture of relief and guilt, the relief only making me feel guiltier. The farther we got from the mountain, the greener the place looked. Until at last it was lost in the morning mist, hidden from our view, like Eden after the fall.

Two weeks after I arrived home, I was shocked to find Jack standing at my front door. He and Ray intended to make good on their plan to stay for the entire summer. But one morning they returned to the cabin after a trip to town to find that someone had fired rifle shots into the front porch. They probably wouldn't have thought anything of it if a storekeeper hadn't told them how he overheard someone talking about "getting the hippies" living on Decker's Mountain. That night the two of them hid behind the couch because they thought they saw headlights coming up the mountain road. They armed themselves with kitchen utensils, certain they could hear footsteps on the front porch. The two of them left the next day, hitchhiking through three states to get home.

I could not know it at the time, but all of this was good training for the pilgrim's life. It taught me that, one way or another, we must all leave Eden behind this side of heaven. I have often come to places I hope will be paradise, only to discover its mansions are too small and its sidewalks have crumbled. There have been rare occasions when something does not fall short of my expectation, a job I love, a place that feels more like home than my real home, or a community as dear to me as family. But the day inevitably comes when the path turns and I must strike the tent and set off down the mountain.

I am only a traveler in the end and cannot help but leave behind a trail of dust and tears. Along the way, I sometimes find myself casting a longing glance over the shoulder and wishing for what once was or wondering what might have been. In my mind's eye I see the light receding in the distance and fear it is the flaming sword of paradise, left as a warning that the way is now forever closed to me. But it isn't. It is only the light of memory. A beacon placed along the path by a loving God for weary pilgrims, left there as a reminder to all who might otherwise be tempted to settle down. It is his way of telling me that I am still on the road and am bound for my true home in heaven.

CHAPTER 8

The Least of These

The Lost Coin was really just a small shed attached to Glad Tidings, a small Pentecostal church near my parents' home. It was furnished with old wooden spools once used for telephone wire. They were turned on their side and covered with checkered table-cloths. Each table had its own votive candle decorated with a picture of praying hands or a Hispanic Jesus with his hand raised in blessing, as if he were flashing the Lost Coin's patrons the peace sign, and his sacred heart bared for all to see. The walls were covered with dark paneling and posters. One warned, "A day without Jesus is a day without the Son." It was dimly lit, except for the small stage where the musicians played. Covered with the remnant of someone's shag carpeting, it looked like it was covered with fur.

There was never much of a crowd at the Lost Coin. Almost any night of the week a handful of regulars sat at the spool tables or huddled at the counter talking quietly. To prove its right to call itself a coffeehouse, the Lost Coin actually served coffee. The strong but otherwise undistinguished brew simmered continually in a large percolator brought over from the church's basement. The place was open seven days a week. It offered music and preaching on Saturday night and fellowship on the other days of the week. I began attending the Lost Coin coffeehouse back in the early seventies, long before the idea of a coffeehouse became synonymous with Starbucks.

Dave, the Jesus freak who gave me the tract at the Jack-in-the-Box, was the Lost Coin's chief prophet. A moment came in nearly every service when he became the mouthpiece of God. On some occasions we were forewarned that the Spirit was about to descend upon him by some physical cue—perhaps a sharp intake of breath or a change in vocal pitch. At other times there were no preliminaries. Dave simply broke into prophetic utterance. Still, we always knew when God took control of Dave, because his vocabulary changed. Suddenly his speech was peppered with "thee," "thou," and the occasional "thus saith the Lord." We did not have to go far to know this was the Spirit speaking through Dave. Our own King James Bibles proved this was the vernacular of God.

Although Dave served as our primary oracle, he was not the only one who claimed to speak for God. One Saturday night a stranger named Lou attended the meeting and midway through Dave's sermon stood up. He lifted his hand, as if he were pronouncing a benediction, and began to prophesy. I was suspicious, but his message bore the trademark King James language. He concluded with a flourish which implied to us that he might possess the prophetic gift to a greater degree than Dave—he collapsed, sending the metal folding chairs around him flying with a loud crash. The overall effect was very convincing. Dave never did anything like this. The newcomer, on the other hand, did so frequently. In fact, the Spirit never seemed to move on him unless there was a pile of metal chairs nearby into which he could fall. It became his trademark.

Dave and Lou teamed up, often prophesying in tandem. Most of the time their messages were simply paraphrases of the Psalms or other passages from the Scriptures: "Thus saith the Lord, I am coming soon. Be bold and courageous, for I will never fail thee nor forsake thee." They could, however, be very specific.

One Saturday night after the meeting several of us decided to go for a ride and "let the Spirit lead" us. Dave drove, and Lou rode shotgun. The two compared their impressions of the Lord's leading as we drove.

"I feel that the Lord wants us to take Gratiot," Dave said.

Lou concurred.

Gratiot was the main drag on our side of town. Turn left and we traveled into the city. Turn right and we went deeper into the suburbs. I was relieved when Dave turned right. It was clear to me that God didn't want us to go into the city. After all, it was nearly midnight. Who knows what kind of people might be out at that time?

We couldn't have gone much more than a mile when Lou interrupted. My heart fell when I heard him say, "I think the Lord wants us to turn around and go in the other direction."

I didn't like the idea, but who was I to argue? They were being led by the Lord. As far as I could tell from what I read in the Bible, God had a habit of asking people to do things they did not want to do and sending them to places they did not want to go. Hadn't he sent Moses back to Egypt against his will? Didn't he command Jonah to go to Nineveh, and hadn't he told Abraham to kill his only son?

We drove deeper into the night and closer to what I was certain was imminent death. I noted with silent dread the moment we passed Eight Mile Road, the line separating the city from the suburbs, and thought about my father's personal conviction never to cross that boundary again. He made this resolution after the nightmare of 1967, when the city of Detroit erupted in race riots. We were visiting relatives at the time and watched the glow of the city's self-immolation from across the lake. It flashed in the night sky like the northern lights. Later I learned my best friend's father handed him the family rifle and told him to shoot anyone who came to the door. Fortunately, no one did.

Now the Holy Spirit was prompting Dave and Lou to drive into the city of Detroit in the middle of the night. There could be only one reason. He planned to make us martyrs.

Barely able to keep the trembling out of my voice, I asked Dave and Lou whether they were absolutely certain this was the way the Lord wanted them to go. "Because I sort of think he wanted us to go in the other direction," I ventured.

They were sure.

Soon the lights of the city came into view.

We parked the car near the bus station and started to roam the streets. Dave and Lou were debating what the Holy Spirit wanted us to do next. Their impasse was broken when one of them tripped over the crumpled form of a man slumped in a doorway. He appeared to be unconscious. The doorway smelled rank with the combined odors of liquor and urine. We gathered around the man and tried to wake him up.

"Hey, brother, are you all right?" someone asked as we tugged at him.

The man sat up and mumbled something unintelligible.

"Are you sick?"

The man mumbled again and slumped back onto the pavement.

Lou was jubilant. "I knew it!" he said. "He's the reason the Lord told us to come here."

"What's your name, brother?" Dave asked.

His answer was slurred, but it sounded like "George."

"Do you need some money, George?" Dave asked. George muttered to himself and closed his eyes.

We decided he might be more responsive if we bought him a cup of coffee. We pulled him to his feet and supported him as we made our way to the bus station, where a few weary travelers sat on benches loaded down with luggage, and a menagerie of street people sought refuge for the night. We got George some coffee and tried to learn more about him. He claimed to be from Germany, where he worked as an engineer. He didn't have any family in the area or a place to stay for the night.

We got out our wallets and pooled our funds. The man looked at the wad of money being offered to him, then apprehensively at a group of gangbangers loitering nearby. "Naw," he said. "Never mind." He just wanted us to leave him alone.

Unable to understand his reluctance, we continued to press him to take our money. Clearly, we were agents of the Lord sent to bless him.

"What are we going to do with him?" Dave asked. "We can't just leave him here."

"We could take him back to the coffeehouse," Lou suggested.

As we left the bus station with George, an unfamiliar voice behind me asked, "Want to know why he wouldn't take your money?" Looking over my shoulder, I saw a new member in our entourage. A skinny young man in a black leather jacket took up the rear and followed us out the door.

"Did you notice those guys over there?" he asked, pointing to the gang.

I said I hadn't realized they were watching us.

"Oh, they were watching you all right," he said.

Clearly they were eyeing us as we made our way out of the bus station.

"You shouldn't flash so much money in public. You never know who is watching."

As he said this, I realized they weren't the only ones who noticed we had money. This stranger had noticed as well. He was starting to make me feel uncomfortable.

The stranger said his name was Mike and he could tell we were Jesus people. He said he was a Jesus freak too and pointed to a cross made of metal studs pressed into his bell-bottom jeans.

"Do you know what would have happened to him if he had taken your money?" Mike asked. I admitted that I didn't.

He smiled and said, "They would have followed him out of the bus station. As soon as he got a few blocks from here, they would have jumped him for it." Then, almost as an afterthought, he added, "Probably would have killed him too."

I began to sweat, wondering what kept them from doing the same to us. The stranger must have read my mind.

"Don't worry," he said. "I kept my eye on them. I let them think I was with you and made sure they saw this before we left." Suddenly, the large blade of a knife appeared in his hand. He flashed it in the streetlight and then closed it with a smirk. "I'll stay in the rear, in case they decide to sneak up on us from behind," Mike said.

We bundled George into the car and headed back to the suburbs. When we got to the Lost Coin, we discussed George's future.

"He's going to need someplace to stay," Dave said.

"Couldn't he just stay here at the coffeehouse?" Lou wondered.

Dave didn't think the church would go for the idea.

"I suppose he could spend the night at my place," Lou reluctantly conceded. "But we need to get him a place of his own. He needs a shower and a change of clothes too!" George did not participate in our deliberations. He simply hung his head and waited for us to decide. Lou looked at me and said, "You look like you're his size. Why don't you find him some of your clothes to wear?"

I went home and looked through my closet. I found a new Levi's shirt and pair of pants, purchased a few days earlier. I liked them and they were fairly expensive, at least for someone working at a fast-food restaurant. I really didn't want to give those away. But as I sorted through my clothes the words of Matthew 25:40 came to mind: "Whatever you did for one of the least of these brothers of mine, you did for me." I wanted Jesus to have my best shirt.

Dave and Lou showed up at Glad Tidings the next day with George in tow now freshly washed and shaved and smartly dressed in a new Levi's shirt and pair of slacks. Perhaps that is why, when they went to the pastor before the service and asked for money to help George get back on his feet, the pastor declined. "There are other organizations better equipped to help him than we are," he explained.

Dave was disappointed, but Lou was furious. At the conclusion of the worship service, he rose to his feet. "I have just one thing to say," Lou declared. "I was hungry and you gave me nothing to eat, I was thirsty and you gave me nothing to drink." Then, turning to George, he said, "Come on, let's get out of here."

Several in the congregation, troubled by what his criticism implied, followed him to the door. "Wait ... wait," they pleaded. "We didn't know anything about it." Lou took an impromptu offering on the spot and collected several hundred dollars. He left the church chuckling.

On Monday, Lou took George to sign him up for public assistance. He got him a cheap apartment and a phone. He planned to pick him up and bring him to the Lost Coin the following Saturday.

By the time Saturday arrived, however, George had disappeared, but I was pretty sure I knew where he was. Back on the street. Dressed in my new shirt and pants and lying in some doorway smelling of urine and vomit.

For the next couple of months, Lou continued his prophetic ministry at the Lost Coin, declaring the word of the Lord and sending chairs flying. The last time I saw him, he came to the restaurant where I worked with a young woman in tow. She looked nervous.

"John," he asked. "How much money do you have on you?"

Shocked by the bluntness of his request, I told him.

"How much do you have in the bank?" he asked.

Still stunned, I told him. It wasn't much. "Give me what you have in your wallet," he ordered. "You can get more for yourself from the bank." He pointed to the girl. "She's broke. Hasn't had anything to eat for a while. I'm broke too."

Something didn't feel quite right. But I thought of Jesus' condemnation: "I was hungry and you gave me nothing to eat, I was thirsty and you gave me nothing to drink, I was a stranger and you did not invite me in, I needed clothes and you did not clothe me, I was sick and in prison and you did not look after me."

I gave him the money in my wallet.

A few weeks later Dave told me that Lou had walked away from his prophetic ministry. He was "backslidden." Lou stopped coming to the Lost Coin and moved in with the girl he brought to the restaurant. He had already been sleeping with her for some time when he asked me for money.

Since then, I have often wondered how Jesus must have viewed our little adventure. Clearly, the pastor was right in not committing the church's funds to such a scheme. George's problems were too complex to think a few dollars from the offering plate could solve them. He was also right in assuming there were other organizations better equipped to help. Perhaps the pastor suspected, as I now do, that Lou was using George's misfortune to run a scam. I have learned through painful experience there are many people who try to take advantage of Jesus' good words and the church's good nature. Some make their living moving like gypsies from place to place, telling churches the same hard-luck story and living off their charity. I see now how we were being naive and foolish. But in some small way we were also wise.

There is no special virtue in being the victim of another's greed or selfishness. Still, Jesus promised that when the Son of Man comes in his glory, no action done on his behalf will go unnoticed. Even a cup of water given in good faith will have its own reward (Matt. 10:42).

On that day the most rewarded will be those who least expect it.

"Lord, when did we see you hungry and feed you, or thirsty and give you something to drink?" they will ask. "When did we see you a stranger and invite you in, or needing clothes and clothe you? When did we see you sick or in prison and go to visit you?"

Jesus will reply, "I tell you the truth, whatever you did for one of the least of these brothers of mine, you did for me."

Looking back at the Christian I once was, I cannot help but admire the kind of faith that took Jesus at his word with such stark simplicity. I do not think I would do so today. My faith has become too sophisticated. My exegesis is too complex. I look at the world through clearer eyes. Eyes too clear, perhaps, to recognize any longer who might qualify as "the least of these."

CHAPTER 9

Dancer

The old man at the concert was dancing.

Furiously.

His feet were a blur in the grass. He snapped his fingers to the music and waved his hands in the air above him. With his face turned heavenward as if in worship, he wore a blissful grin. The man moved up toward the band and then back toward the crowd. Up toward the band. Back toward the crowd. Again and again. Some in the crowd smiled. A few snickered. I felt embarrassed for him.

"Check him out," I muttered to my wife, Jane. "I wonder if he thinks he looks cool?"

Something about the old man's spontaneity brought Carl to mind. I hadn't thought of him for years. Carl wasn't a dancer. Carl fancied himself to be a singer. He wasn't like the rest of us. He was the kind of person we used to refer to as slow. In fact, he could be somewhat embarrassing at times. He talked a little too loud. Sometimes he laughed too hard at our jokes. And there were the songs. Good Lord, the songs!

Carl worked as part of the cleaning crew at a restaurant washing dishes. The work wasn't hard but the company he kept as he carried it out was. In those days people who were slow weren't "special," they were just retarded. That is how Carl's fellow employees regarded him, as "that retarded kid" who did the dishes.

We like to believe people who are slow don't know what we think about them. But they do. Carl heard the snickers behind his back and got the jokes. He knew when other people were making fun of him. Sometimes, when he knew they weren't looking, he went off by himself and wept.

I don't know when Carl started attending the Lost Coin. He was already a regular when I showed up at the door. At first, I was a little put off by him. Usually, I saw his sort only from a distance. In school, people like Carl were segregated from the rest of us, relegated to the special-education class in school. They sat at their own lunch table. We "normal" folks did not have to be bothered with them.

Well, there was one other person. There was Joe. A member of the Baptist church where I attended the Wednesday night children's club, Joe lived at the YMCA and worked as a janitor. He had a telephone "ministry," calling the clubbers each week to see how they were doing. Conversations with him were long and awkward.

"How're you doin' tonight?" he asked.

"Okay," I said, hoping he would hang up if I didn't say too much. But Joe was persistent.

"Sure is a cold one out there, isn't it?"

"Yep."

"It's so cold, I'm wearing my long underwear. How about you?"

I finally told Joe to stop calling. He was hurt, unable to understand why I didn't want to talk to him.

Carl reminded me of Joe. He was friendly enough, all right. But hard to talk to. I felt awkward around him. I suppose, deep inside, I wanted him to go away. But I had read my Bible. I knew the sort of people God chooses for his own. God chooses the foolish things of the world to shame the wise and the weak things of the world to shame the strong. He chooses the lowly and despised. The wise need the foolish, and the strong need the weak. If there were no place in the body of Christ for a person like Carl, I reasoned, there might well be no place in it for a person like me.

The others at the coffeehouse did not seem as uncomfortable with Carl. He was almost a kind of mascot to them, but not in a condescending way. He was a symbol to them of God's grace. The simplicity of his faith appealed to them. They also admired his boldness. Whatever Carl's limitation may have been, it did not keep him from sharing his faith with others. I don't think he ever visited the coffeehouse without a testimony of some opportunity to tell someone else about the love of Jesus Christ. Carl often witnessed to people at work, the same people who ridiculed him so often. In one breath he described with tears the mean things they said or did to him, and in the next, he told us how he gave them the gospel.

Whatever else Carl was, he was an evangelist. He talked to friends and strangers alike and was unashamed. Where the gospel was concerned, he was fearless. I could not say the same for myself.

But Lord, couldn't you have done something about those songs?

Carl did not play a musical instrument. I suppose I would have preferred it if he had. I played a little guitar and could sing a bit. Not as well as most of the others who provided special music at the Lost Coin, of course, but passably enough to perform a duet once in a while and receive a smattering of applause when it was over.

The only instrument Carl had to offer God was his voice. It was not a particularly pleasant voice either. It ranged up and down some obscure scale known only to Carl. It had a pitch all its own. It did not matter what the melody line was, Carl was always a half step above or below it. It wasn't so bad when we sang as a group; we could usually drown him out. But Carl liked to sing solos.

Every few weeks Carl asked to do special music at the coffeehouse. He usually sang without accompaniment. Sometimes the number he performed bore a vague resemblance to one of the songs in the songbooks. Frequently, however, he performed his own compositions, songs he made up right there on the spot. These were songs that, as he put it, the Lord gave him. In fact, the Lord appeared to give them to Carl in the very moment he sang them. When Carl opened his mouth, even he did not know what might come out.

Some of Carl's songs were hybrids. He began with the words of a hymn we all knew sung to a melody we couldn't recognize and then, like a jazz singer, improvised new stanzas of his own.

"Sweet little Jesus boy," he sang one Christmas, "we didn't know who you were."

He sang until the words no longer came, which at times felt like ten minutes or more. The song went on and on, so long that I prayed for him to stop.

"God," I pleaded, "Carl says you are giving this song to him. Please stop. And if you're not giving him the words, make him stop."

God ignored my prayer.

Not only did Carl sing words and melodies known only to himself, making it impossible for the rest of us to add our voices to the proceedings, he also sang with abandon. Carl sang with feeling. So much feeling it embarrassed me. Didn't he know what he sounded like? Didn't he realize everybody could tell he made the songs up as he went along? Couldn't he feel our, or at least my, discomfort with the whole thing?

The answer was no, he did not. When Carl sang, he lost touch with the rest of us. This was not a performance. It was worship in its rawest form. We may have called it special music, but Carl sang for a different audience than the one we intended. His music was geared for the halls of heaven, the one who sits on the throne, and the countless angels that bow in his presence. What did he care about the feelings of mere mortals like me?

Carl's worship was like the dancing of King David when he brought up the ark of the Lord from the house of Obed-Edom to Jerusalem. David danced, the Scripture says, "with all his might." In other words, David danced with abandon. He must have, too, because he stripped off his outer garment and danced while dressed only in a linen ephod. Imagine how shocked your church might be if next Sunday someone worshiped God with an energy that generated so much heat they stripped down to their underwear! It isn't exactly the same. David wore a linen garment similar to the priests. But the overall effect was the same. David's wife later told him that he might as well have been naked.

It must have been a long dance too. They sacrificed a bull and a fattened calf every six steps. While David danced, the people shouted, the trumpets blared, and his wife Michal, a daughter of royalty, looked on with contempt. "How the king of Israel has distinguished himself today," she sneered, "disrobing in the sight of the slave girls of his servants as any vulgar fellow would!"

The criticism did not bother David.

"It was before the LORD, who chose me rather than your father or anyone from his house when he appointed me ruler over the LORD's people Israel—I will celebrate before the LORD," he retorted. "I will become even more undignified than this, and I will be humiliated in my own eyes. But by these slave girls you spoke of, I will be held in honor" (2 Sam. 6:21–22).

That was Carl's philosophy too. He sang with the same kind of abandon that David must have displayed in his dance. He didn't care who was watching. "If you don't like it," he seemed to say, "then you can lump it. I am performing for an audience of one."

Whatever Carl was, he was not ashamed. He was not ashamed to worship. He was not ashamed to witness. More than anything else, he was not ashamed of Jesus. I could not always say the same of myself.

Perhaps that is why Carl sometimes annoyed me. Something about the way he abandoned himself so unself-consciously to worship made me self-conscious. When he sang I could not help being aware of myself and of the audience. This was one of the reasons I wanted him to stop. I was too aware of myself—the music wasn't to my taste. I was too aware of the audience—the style didn't reflect the kind of professionalism or poise that attracted others to our services. I wasn't worried about what God thought of his worship. It was all about what others might think. There was more of Michal than David in me.

Not Carl, though. I do not think he would have stopped singing even if he knew I objected.

Which is why the old man at the concert brought him to mind.

My wife and I were attending a performance by a Beatles tribute band in a nearby park. The audience spread across the lawn, listening sedately on blankets and in lawn chairs. Then the band struck up the notes of "Twist and Shout." After the first few bars I noticed a figure snaking his way through the audience until he was in front of the band. He was an elderly gentleman, perhaps in his late sixties, tanned and smartly dressed in a pair of khakis and a Polo shirt. He looked like he might have been quite a ladies' man in his younger days. He shuffled his feet, like a man doing the soft shoe, and grinned away. I looked at Jane and rolled my eyes.

When the song ended, the man made his way back to his seat. But he wasn't done. A few minutes later we could see him moving toward the front again, his feet flying and his fingers snapping. My wife and I rolled our eyes at each other. Couldn't he tell how foolish he looked? Didn't he care? At last, he finished, acknowledged the applause, and went back to his seat.

"I wonder how much he's had to drink tonight," someone said. At least he was finished.

Or so we thought. When the unmistakable chords to "Roll Over Beethoven" sounded, the man was on his feet again. By now he clearly felt a sense of ownership. He danced with the same abandon each time, alternately smiling at the audience and then up to heaven, as if God were his dancing partner and he were giving him a nod of approval for his performance. When he finished, he waved toward the band and then lifted his hand heavenward, as if passing any accolades for his performance on to them and to God. Something about the way he did it made me think of those Christian performers who point skyward whenever they receive applause.

I thought of David. Then I thought of Carl.

I probably wouldn't have given the event another thought if not for an odd coincidence. A week after the concert in the park, my wife and I attended a Christian music festival in another state. A kind of Woodstock for believers, the festival included several tents with a wide variety of music. Jane and I planted ourselves in the "folk" tent while my two boys went off to listen to their heavy metal and hardcore bands. The announcer described the group we were listening to as a "rockabilly" band.

I didn't like them. I was pretty much waiting for their set to end when another old man began to gyrate his way through the crowd and move toward the stage. He flailed his legs in time to the beat and whipped his arms out in front of him, all the while flashing a wide yellow grin. Every few seconds he threw his arms into the air in an obvious gesture of praise and spread his palms out as if in supplication to the Lord. The crowd around him smiled approvingly, but no one else joined him in the dance.

The man did this once, twice, and then three times, oblivious of the audience. There was only the music and the dance. And God in heaven, who looked on.

CHAPTER 10

Soon, but Not Too Soon

Jesus came back on a Saturday night. Mike and I were sitting in his car after prayer meeting and talking about the Bible. Mike was another of the regulars at the Lost Coin. We talked about the return of Christ and said it could happen that very night. The remark wasn't prompted by any single event or sign. The meeting had not been remarkable. In fact, there wasn't anything especially different about this particular Saturday night that led us to make such an observation. We said the same thing every Saturday night.

I was a new Christian at the time and only recently learned about the return of Christ. My friends spoke of it as "the rapture," a strange term which sounded more suitable for a romance novel than for religion. The rapture, they explained, was when Jesus will return to collect his church shortly before the second coming. They found this teaching in the Bible, in Paul's first letter to the Thessalonians, and in the very mysterious book of Revelation. I'd read Revelation, the last book of the Bible, and was unable to make much sense of it. It was filled with plagues, weird creatures, and strange visions of heaven. I did not doubt its truth. I simply took it at face value.

Now, it seemed, the rapture had arrived. It came just as Mike started to read a verse from his Bible. He was cut off midsentence by a howl that sounded like something from beyond the grave. At first it began soft and low, barely registering on our consciousness, but soon built to an eerie crescendo. Mike and I nodded as we looked at each other in wide-eyed amazement. This could be only one thing. It must be the "last trump," the shout of the archangel calling us into Christ's presence.

The eerie call continued to sound as Mike and I sat in his car and waited to be caught up into glory in the blink of an eye. I felt an initial wave of relief because I was fully clothed and talking about the Bible when Jesus returned. That should look pretty good on my record. I might have felt less assured had I considered Jesus probably viewed such thoughts as evidence of spiritual pride.

Mike began to pray. I followed suit, but with less confidence. We had blinked several times since the "trump" began to sound. If this was Jesus coming for his saints, he had either overlooked us or decided to leave us behind. Like a driver whose car has stalled and hopes he can get it started with a push, I began to bounce in my seat hoping one of them would take.

What began as a clear tone ended in a piercing howl that made the hair on the back of my head stand on end. As the sound trailed off in the night, I blushed to realize its true source. It did not emanate from heaven or hell but from the dog next door. We would have to wait another day for Jesus to come.

I was disappointed ... and relieved. My ambivalence about Christ's return was fueled partially by the way this doctrine was sometimes presented. There were times when the prospect of the imminent return of Christ was held over my head as a potential threat. Those who spoke of the nearness of Christ's coming did so with the kind of grim satisfaction a mother might have when warning her erring child, "Wait until your father gets home!"

I noticed Jesus, too, spoke of his coming in terms that sometimes sounded like a veiled threat. He said it will come upon people without warning. He warned that some will be taken and others left behind. But he implied it would be preferable to be among those who will be caught up. Somehow the preachers I heard made either alternative sound like a threat. What if we were in the theater when Jesus returned? How, they wanted to know, would we explain ourselves to him?

These were sobering questions, to be sure. But I was troubled by a more pragmatic concern. I was worried because I did not normally sleep in pajamas. What if Jesus came back in the middle of the night, like the bridegroom in the parable of the ten virgins? I did not relish the thought of suddenly appearing before the heavenly host in my shorts. Far better to be among the dead, who do not have to concern themselves with such matters. They leave their bodies behind when they are called into the presence of God. Those who will be caught up in the rapture take their bodies with them. Nervous about the possibility of embarrassment when that day came, I started wearing my jeans to bed.

I soon realized that even with these measures, there were other possible contingencies for which I was unable to prepare. What if I happened to be taking a shower when the rapture came? I could wear a bathing suit in the shower, but there was always the possibility Jesus might come in that moment after I changed out of my clothes and before I put my suit on. The Bible says those who will be taken in the rapture will go up in the twinkling of an eye. I didn't think I could change that fast, and I wasn't sure Jesus would wait.

My anxiety was alleviated somewhat when I learned the martyrs in heaven will be given white robes to wear. God, I was told, had a robe for me too. Although I felt a little better knowing this, it sounded like I would spend eternity in pajamas. I didn't normally wear a robe either.

I was afraid I would not be ready for Jesus when he came. My friends believed that Christians who aren't "right with the Lord" at the time of the rapture will remain on earth during the tribulation while the rest of the church is caught up. They considered this an incentive for holy living. Since the Lord's return could come at any moment, it was best to keep one's accounts short — very short. But it was hard for me to be motivated by this kind of teaching, because I was never sure how to determine the threshold when someone was no longer "right."

I could see how murderers and rapists who claimed to be Christians might have a problem, but the people I knew who were worried about being left behind didn't fall into those categories. They were pretty much like me. How could I be sure I was in a proper state of grace? I went forward every week when the altar call was given, searching my soul and agonizing over my lack of commitment. I didn't pray enough. I didn't witness enough. I wasn't obedient enough. But how much was enough? Nobody could tell me.

I knew I was supposed to look forward to Jesus' return. But I wasn't sure I wanted him to come too quickly. Barely out of high school with most of life left to experience, I still had many things I wanted to try before leaving earth behind. I felt guilty for thinking such things. Jesus warned that at the time of his coming, people will be eating and drinking, marrying and giving in marriage. He did not mean this as a compliment.

Most of the Christians I knew led lives that weren't much different from anyone else's. They went to school and to work. They had wives and sweethearts. They got married and had children. On weekends they washed their cars and did yard work. Once in a while someone took a stab at radical commitment by refusing to buy life insurance. A few of my friends questioned whether it was right for Christians living in the last days to date or marry, considering the mundane necessities of married life to be too much of a distraction. Most lived normal lives. I wasn't sure how it was possible to avoid the concerns of earthly life. It was the only life I knew.

I soon discovered I was not the only one who was concerned about such things. With the look of a man who has been invited to a very dull party and knows he cannot refuse, my best friend confided that he was worried about heaven.

"I know we're supposed to look forward to being in heaven more than being on earth," he explained. "But when I read the book of Revelation, it looks like all we will be doing is bowing up and down." "Up and down," he repeated in a note of despair. "Up and down, for all eternity!"

I tried to reassure him that eternity would be more interesting than earth, but I shared his reservations. God seemed to have left the most exciting aspects of earthly life out of heaven. For example, I knew there was no marriage in heaven and, I assumed, no sex either. I could see a pragmatic reason for such exclusions. There is no need for procreation in a place where eternal life is the norm. But heaven included other elements of earthly life that were just as superfluous. I was told our time in eternity begins with a great banquet. In my opinion, eating was as unnecessary as sex to those who have eternal life, and not nearly as interesting. From what I read in the book of Revelation, there also appeared to be a lot of falling down and casting of crowns. I didn't normally wear a hat, so the prospect of handling crowns wasn't very motivating to me.

I could tell that singing, too, was an important feature of heavenly existence. This didn't surprise me. But I worried about the style of music. When I first began to attend church regularly, I was nervous about the sermon and even more about singing. As the organist played the introduction to the first hymn, the man next to me gave me a reassuring grin and pointed to the place in the hymnal. I listened to the first stanza and hesitantly joined in for the second. Beaming at me, my neighbor nodded and said, "That's what I like best about this music—you don't have to know it to sing it. After one verse you can sing just about anything."

He was right. The hymns weren't very difficult. One consisted of a single word, "alleluia," sung repeatedly for an interminable length of time. When I sang "every day with Jesus is sweeter than the day before," I tried to measure whether this was really true for me. Some days were the same as the day before. Others seemed a little worse. When I sang "At the Cross" and came to the line that says, "Now I am happy all the day," it bothered me that this wasn't the case with me.

It made me nervous when the pastor grumbled about people who found church boring. He wondered aloud about what they thought we would be doing for all eternity. I wondered the same, but for a different reason. I was afraid there would not be enough to hold my interest for that long. C. S. Lewis observed that joy is the serious business of heaven, but I did not find much joy in the church. There were moments of exhilaration when I felt caught up in a stanza of a hymn or the preacher's words made me feel as if I were under the scrutiny of God. But most of the time it was uneventful, if not a little boring.

Meanwhile joy, like the day of the Lord, had a habit of showing up unexpectedly, as if it were a thief intent on catching me unaware. It stole up on me at inexplicable and inopportune moments — while driving in the car or making the bed — only to vanish as soon as I became aware of its presence. When I looked for it on my own, particularly in church, it eluded me. Later on, my reading of Lewis helped me to understand that this is often the way of joy. A glimpse of heaven refracted through the shadows of earthly experience, joy prefers to inhabit the periphery of our spiritual vision. It is spare in its frequency and as demure as a virgin on her wedding night.

In time my anxiety about heaven diminished somewhat as I continued to study the Bible. I began to see that many of the images the Scriptures use to speak of heaven are intentionally earthly, employing the language of the ordinary to describe the eternal. The appearance of the angelic beings that surround the throne of God combines elements common to earthly creatures, making them terrifying in their familiarity. The architecture of heaven, according to Scripture, is rife with beautiful gems and precious metals.

Some view these descriptions as symbolic, used by the writers of Scripture to speak of an indescribable reality. Others are adamant that they are literal. I suspect they are both. I would not be surprised to find there are real robes and crowns in eternity. But there is surely more to these images than meets the eye. C. S. Lewis explains the necessity for this: "Heaven is, by definition, outside our experience, but all intelligible descriptions must be of things within our experience." Earthly experience is the only experience we know and must be our starting point when speaking of heaven.

I should not have been surprised. This was true for me before I ever read a word of the Bible. My earliest memory is of being seated in a green field littered with yellow flowers. The grassy carpet stretches infinitely in every direction, its vastness the very definition of eternity. Awash in the glory of it, I feel carried away by its beauty, the way a swimmer might be borne on the rolling waves of some vast ocean. Nearby an unseen presence watches over me with loving interest. I realize now the green field of my memory was actually the weedy lawn behind the small suburban home where I grew up. The lovely flowers were dandelions. The loving presence who watched over me so keenly was my mother. This is the first mental image that shaped my idea of what heaven might be like.

A childhood visit to an old farm provided the other image that shaped my earliest notion of heaven. We entered the house through the back door, the entrance reserved for friends. I sat at a table covered with a red checkered cloth and listened to the adults converse. The kitchen walls were bright with sunlight as it beamed through the window. I remember thinking I wanted to live in an old house when I grew up, near friends who came knocking at my back door to visit. Yet if I had, I am certain it would have fallen short of my expectation, just as no field of flowers has ever been able to match the beauty of the summer lawn I remember from my infancy.

This is the mystery of the earthly images God uses to point us to heaven. They speak to us of our final destination but cannot take us there. The earthly images do not say all that can be said and much of what could be said cannot be put into human language. At least, not yet. These earthly images carry the fragrance of heaven with them, but that is all. Those who seek heaven in the images themselves find only dust and ashes.

The best these images can do is to provide us with a rudimentary descriptive vocabulary. They are figures intended to help us to anticipate what is to come. But it is a limited vocabulary. The Bible draws on our experience to paint a picture that mirrors the true reality of heaven, but only in broad strokes. We do not see its towers and spires with clarity. Rather, we see "through a glass darkly," a poor reflection in a dim mirror. Perhaps the fault, if there is one, lies with human language. It is too narrow a pallette to hold all the colors of heaven. We who have not experienced heaven cannot know what it is truly like. If Lewis is right that language must use human experience as its point of reference, then the images of the Bible can move only in one direction. They argue from the lesser to the greater by using the known to describe the unknown.

Ultimately, however, the problem is with us. Sin has made us innately incredulous when it comes to the realities of heaven. Jesus' criticism of Nicodemus in John 3:12 is equally true of us: "I have spoken to you of earthly things and you do not believe; how then will you believe if I speak of heavenly things?" There is a high likelihood that we would not believe, even if the language could be found to tell us.

When my oldest son, Drew, was a small child, Jane found him in the living room playing with a plastic bag. Seeing he was about to put it over his head, she reprimanded him, explaining that what he wanted to do was very dangerous. Drew, of course, wanted to know why. She told him he might suffocate and die. This was Drew's first encounter with the notion of death.

As Jane considered what to say next, I thought back to my childhood and the moment when I learned about death for the first time. Arnold, one of my father's coworkers, had suffered a heart attack. As my father was about to leave for the funeral home, I asked if I could ride along. My parents didn't think it was a good idea. I had never been in a funeral home before or seen a corpse. Death was a stranger to me. Their reticence only intrigued me more. I asked more questions about my father's friend and his fate.

"He'll come back to work after the funeral, right?" I asked.

My father chuckled sadly. "No, Johnny, he won't."

"Why not?" I asked.

"Because his heart stopped beating. He's dead."

"But it will start again, won't it?"

"No, it won't."

I found this hard to accept. I was even more disturbed when I learned my father's friend was to be buried in the ground.

"He won't be back at all? Ever?" I was incredulous that such a thing could take place.

"Nope," my father replied, in a cavalier tone. "When you're dead, you're dead. That's it."

Without the hope of the gospel, there was little else he could say. Although he tried to make light of it, his simple statement shook me to my core and changed the way I looked at the world around me. Like a patient who has just been informed by the doctor that his condition is terminal, I realized he had just pronounced my own death sentence. What was true of my father's friend must also be true of me. One day I too would die. They would lay my body out in a funeral home and then place it in the ground. I sobbed when I realized this, consumed with grief, not for my father's friend but for myself.

Just as Adam died on the day when he partook of the fruit from the tree of the knowledge of good and evil, something died in me when I realized he was telling the truth. From that moment on, the prospect of death dogged my heels, as relentless as any predator in pursuit of its prey. I became conscious of the passage of time, any enjoyment now tempered by knowing it was only fleeting. The passing of each event signaled the approaching end like the tolling of a bell. The end of the game gave way to the end of the party. The end of summer gave way to the end of the year. The end of the year would, in time, give way to the end of my life.

Jane did not want our son to bear such a burden, so she tried to explain the concept of death coupled with the hope of heaven. Using language that a small child could understand, she told Drew she did not want him to die, but that he did not have to fear death.

"When you die," she gently explained, "you will go to be with Jesus in heaven."

Drew thought about this for a moment, then began to sob inconsolably.

"Who will take care of me in heaven?" he wailed.

Jane took him in her arms and comforted him. Wiping the tears from his eyes, she gave him the only answer she could.

"God will," she said.

But these were not the words he wanted to hear.

This is the dilemma we face when it comes to being heavenly minded. It is hard to think of heaven without thinking of earth. Our earthly reality is more tangible. We barely know what awaits us and can't really know what we are missing. "No eye has seen," the apostle Paul assures us, "no ear has heard, no mind has conceived what God has prepared for those who love him" (1 Cor. 2:9). It is hard to wait for what we cannot see. Harder yet to long for what we do not know. Fortunately for us, God has revealed these things to us by his Spirit. Like a bride who is so eager for her wedding night that the faded picture of her lover will kindle the fire of desire, we too are surrounded by images designed to ignite our longing for heaven. They are only shadows and not the reality of the life to come. But for now, they are enough.

CHAPTER 11

Sparrow

Yolanda was a petite beauty with large soulful eyes. She also had a brain tumor that kept her from driving. The regulars at the Lost Coin were "believing God for a miracle," expecting Yolanda to be healed at any moment. In the meantime, she briefly designated me as her unofficial chauffeur.

Yolanda's pixie smile and infectious giggle masked the seriousness of her condition, but the subtle clues were there to be seen by those who knew her. Surgery slurred Yolanda's speech. This, combined with the effects of the medicine she took, gave her voice a sleepy lilt making her sound just a little drunk. Sometimes she had trouble walking up and down steps. She tumbled down the stairway of her home three times.

"You can't imagine how hard it is to walk down the stairs until you have to think about each step as you take it," she once told me.

She was right. I couldn't imagine. The notion of going through life a step at a time was unfathomable to me. I always took the stairs two at a time. Too young to feel the need for a sense of history, I careened through life like a passenger on a fast train whose view of the landscape is no more than a blur of scenery. I was in a hurry, anxious to reach a future that took its own sweet time to arrive.

The same must have been true of Yolanda once. Prior to her illness, the future lay before her like a path one can travel with long and careless strides and still have just as far to go at day's end. Now she made her way with carefully measured steps, sensing the swift approach of journey's end and, after, a long night.

Yolanda was not troubled by the possibility of death. Like us, she asked God to heal her. But if he chose not to, she knew heaven was the alternative because of her faith in Christ. The inconveniences imposed upon her by her condition bothered her more. She missed driving and did not like being dependent upon others to get around. She called me for rides because I worked nights and was the most available person she knew at the time.

She also missed having long hair. She wore a wig after they shaved her head for surgery and didn't like it. Now that her hair was long enough to wear in a short but stylish hairdo, she enjoyed going to the beauty shop. She also liked wearing makeup. One afternoon I took her to buy new makeup and watched her as she put it on and explained the mysterious rites of beauty to me. She said she felt a bit guilty when she used makeup, wondering whether it was vain to spend so much time on her appearance. She thought her sickness might have been God's way of chastising her for the pride she felt about her appearance. This made no sense to me. Why would God create her to be a beauty and then be angry with her for noticing his handiwork?

I did not think much about her cancer. It came to mind only when necessity forced it into my consciousness. I thought of it when she took her medicine. Or when I noticed her carefully making her way down the stairs, giving thought to each step as if it were some kind of philosophical conundrum that must be worked out. Most of the time, she was just like anyone else. How serious could her condition be? At any rate, it did not matter. After all, we were believing God for her healing. It was only a matter of time.

My secret doubt came to the surface when we were in an automobile accident. It was my fault. I picked Yolanda up at her house and took her to lunch. After lunch, she still held her drink in her hand when I turned into the path of an oncoming car. It hit the passenger's side and sent Yolanda lurching toward the driver's seat. Soda pop covered the dashboard and the cup was nowhere to be seen.

The accident was not serious. But the impact of the other vehicle shook Yolanda. She reached instinctively for her head, as if to protect the spot where she bore a scar from her surgery.

I barely noticed. I was more preoccupied by how the accident might affect my insurance rates.

"I can't afford this," I muttered, as I opened the door.

The driver of the other car was angry.

"You turned right in front of me!" he said.

I could not argue with him. I didn't try to explain. I simply apologized, all the while shaking my head and continuing to mutter.

"I can't afford this. I really can't afford this."

Suddenly, the other driver softened. I am not sure why. Perhaps he heard my muttering and took pity on me. Maybe he was charmed by Yolanda's smile and her gentle plea that he let me off without reporting the accident. I suppose he could have mistaken us for a young married couple just getting started in life, rather than the casual friends we were supposed to be. Whatever the reason, his disposition changed. We did not exchange insurance information.

"Be more careful," he admonished as he drove off. I watched in disbelief.

"Praise the Lord!" I sighed.

Relieved and embarrassed, I got back in the car, laughing nervously about the collision. Yolanda, however, was angry.

"You *do* need to be more careful," she said. "I could have been really hurt." She moved her hand on the side of her head again, as if she were trying to shield it from an imagined blow. "Do you realize what could have happened if I'd hit my head against the window?"

My heart sank. Not so much at her reproof, which I knew to be true, but more because of what was implied by its blunt reminder. God hadn't healed her. At least, not yet. Although I wanted to pretend that Yolanda was like any other girl, she was not. The thing we rarely mentioned was still there, perhaps even growing. Her condition was more serious than I wanted to admit.

On one of our excursions I decided to stop by the house and introduce Yolanda to my mother. I am not sure why. She didn't ask to visit my family. She and I were not dating, and when I did go out on dates, I never brought them home. Yet for some reason I wanted Yolanda to meet my mother.

I wonder, now, if it was the child in me that prompted my decision. I sensed how fragile Yolanda really was. Did I bring her home hoping she could be fixed, like the sparrow my brother and sister and I once recovered from a neighbor across the street? Our neighbor found the tiny bird in his attic while renovating his house. Its leg was so tangled in its nest it could not escape. The bird's mother abandoned it and left it there to die.

We brought the helpless thing home to our parents, certain they knew how to fix it. I can't imagine what they must have thought upon hearing our impossible demand. My father was unwilling. There was nothing to be done for the pitiful creature. We children wept. My mother pleaded with him. Finally, he decided radical surgery was the only way to save the bird's life. He cut it away from the nest, amputating its leg. He treated the stump with alcohol and wrapped it in a bandage.

Amazingly, the bird survived the trauma. We kept the sparrow and fed it until it regained its strength. One day the bird spread its wings and took flight. First we rejoiced. Then we wept. For the next few summers we were certain our yard was occasionally visited by a one-legged sparrow who perched on our fence and sang.

Perhaps I wanted Yolanda to meet my mother because she also knew what it was like to have scars. Yolanda's were the result of her battle with cancer. My mother's were emotional, the result of a hard childhood in Depression-era Saskatchewan. Yolanda and my mother shared a waiflike quality that made them tough and vulnerable at the same time. She immediately recognized Yolanda as a kindred spirit and declared her to be a "doll." "She's a real cupcake," she said.

When I came home later that night, she asked, "Is she your girlfriend?" I could tell she hoped the answer was yes.

"Mom! C'mon!" I protested, flushing red with embarrassment. "Why does she have to be my girlfriend? Why can't she just be my friend?"

She grinned in return, "Why couldn't she be your girlfriend?" My mother was amused by my dismay.

She recognized my protest for the lie it was. I was tired of being Yolanda's driver. I wanted to be more than friends. Yolanda saw it too but did not share my feelings.

"I don't think you should drive me around anymore," she said to me one day.

"Why?" I protested. "It's no trouble." That, of course, was also a lie.

With the kind of gentle smile you might give when explaining something to a younger but beloved sibling, she said she was afraid I was developing feelings for her.

"I think you want me to be more than a sister in the Lord," she said.

At first I denied it. Afterward I protested, "What if I did? What would be so bad about that?"

"I'm older than you," she explained. This was true. She was a few years older than me, but no more than two or three at the most.

"I don't think you're too old," I argued.

"I'm more mature in the Lord than you," she continued.

This was also true. But her argument did not convince me. True, I was young in my faith, but I was growing every day. The difference hadn't hindered our spiritual conversations in the past. Why should it be a problem in the future?

"Besides, I'm seeing Dave," she finally said.

Now here was an argument I could not refute. It was her trump card. Everybody at the Lost Coin knew she was dating Dave, the prophet. I knew it too.

"But," I thought to myself, "Dave never seems to have the time to drive you around when you need it. Maybe you ought to start seeing someone else."

I kept the thought to myself.

In fact, Dave had noticed my "ministry" to Yolanda. He did not exactly accuse me of trying to move in on his territory, but one Saturday night he told me he had a word from the Lord for me.

It was couched in the usual scriptural allusions and King James English. Read between the lines, the message was essentially this: "God has a way of dealing with those who steal ... especially those who steal from his prophets." It may have been a word from the Lord, but the voice was all Dave's.

In the end, I could not persuade Yolanda to change her mind. She stopped calling me for rides. Eventually, for other reasons than this, I stopped visiting the Lost Coin. The last time I saw Yolanda was at the worship service at another church. As she walked through the crowd our eyes met, but she looked past me, as if she didn't know me. It had been several months since I had been her driver.

"Yolanda!" I called out as she was about to walk past me.

She stopped and looked at me in momentary confusion. Then she smiled apologetically.

"I used to know you, didn't I?" she asked.

I nodded.

"Were we friends?" she asked.

I hardly knew how to answer.

"I'm sorry," she said. "I had another operation. I've forgotten a lot of the people I used to know. I don't remember your name."

"It's John," I said.

She looked thoughtful for a moment, the way she did when trying to navigate the stairs. Then she smiled again. "Yes. I think I remember you. It's good to see you, John. The Lord bless you." Then she continued on her way.

This is what happens in a world broken by sin. Memory fades, sparrows fall, and we are left behind too soon by those we love. The weight of it would crush us, if it were not for the one who knows every name and has his eye on the sparrow. He has promised he will never forget or forsake us. "Can a mother forget the baby at her breast and have no compassion on the child she has borne?" he asks. "Though she may forget, I will not forget you!" (Isa. 49:15).

Jesus told us no sparrow falls apart from the will of the Father and that every hair on our head is numbered (Matt. 10:29–31). He has promised to be with us to the end of the age (Matt. 28:20).

A few months after I spoke to Yolanda, I met a mutual friend in the park. He grinned widely, as if something wonderful had happened. "Did you hear the news about Yolanda?" he asked.

My heart leaped with anticipation.

"Did she finally get healed?"

"No," he replied, still grinning. "She died! Praise the Lord!"

I must have looked stunned, because he went on to explain why this was such good news.

"Don't you get it, man? She's in heaven!"

He continued to grin at me, waiting for the proper reply.

"Praise the Lord," he said, as if to cue my response.

I forced myself to smile.

"Yeah, praise the Lord," I mumbled.

Blinking back tears, I turned away.

CHAPTER 12

The Prophet of Detroit

Before I was a pastor or a professor, I was a prophet. Not just any prophet, either; I was a prophet greater than Isaiah. At least, that is what I was told. The calling came in the early morning hours at the Lost Coin as a few of us were huddled together for prayer.

We often stayed after the regular meeting, sometimes until 1:00 or 2:00 a.m., hoping to hear a message from the Lord. When they came, these divine "revelations" ranged from sweeping promises of the Lord's soon return to very specific directives.

On one occasion, for example, one of the local prophets told a couple who had recently gone out on their first date that they were to be married. I knew of at least two couples who received similar messages, along with sweeping assurances that God had blessed their unions. Both are divorced today.

Another prophecy informed me the Lord wanted me to quit smoking. This was not exactly a news flash. The surgeon general told me the same thing every day. Dire warnings were inscribed on every pack of Kools I opened. A committed smoker since eighth grade, I tried to quit for months, without much success. This time, for some reason, things were different.

It wasn't because I felt the Lord outranked the surgeon general or because I sensed any threat of divine punishment. I quit because I was anxious about God's reputation. I reasoned if God promised to give me the power to quit and I continued to smoke, the only conclusion to be drawn was that God was a liar and all I based my faith upon was false. There was simply too much at stake. I determined this time to quit for good. I haven't smoked a cigarette since.

I suppose the knowledge that God's awareness of my personal life extended as far as the number of cigarettes I smoked each day should have made me nervous. Instead, I found it encouraging. It was evidence that God is really there. More important, it was proof that God is aware of me, specifically. These two facts lay behind my intense interest in the prophetic gift and the reason I was attracted to the Lost Coin in the first place.

Till now I spent most of my life wondering whether God truly exists. These people acted as if they had just had a conversation with him. They believed he is alive and that he communicates with us today. We stayed up late into the night praying together and hoping to receive messages from him. Some of the messages were odd. One prophecy quoted Matthew 10:30, which says that even the hairs on our head are numbered by God. Aimed at a woman whose husband was not a believer, it promised to bring her husband to a point of faith by causing him to go bald. For some reason it never occurred to us that if such a strategy were effective, half the population would already be saved.

Another person was told God planned to heal his eyesight and he no longer needed his glasses. First, however, he must demonstrate his faith. He threw his glasses out of the car window while on the highway. He still needed them several months later.

My message came in the back room at the Lost Coin. A group of us were gathered in a circle praying when Dave looked at me and said, "The Lord wants to give you a gift, brother." I was thrilled to have been noticed and even more thrilled that I was about to receive a spiritual gift.

"What is it?" I asked.

Dave paused for a moment, looking as though he were listening to someone speaking. I could hear nothing.

"Prophecy," he said at last. That is when he told me I was to be a prophet greater than Isaiah. I was going to speak to kings and princes, rulers and principalities. He said I would crush Satan under my heel.

I was overwhelmed with joy. Of all the spiritual gifts, prophecy was the one I admired most. If I could have chosen a gift for myself, this was the gift I would have selected.

I waited anxiously for something to happen.

Nothing.

No voices.

No signs.

No wonders.

Just silence.

How does one begin a ministry of prophecy? I didn't know. They didn't teach this sort of thing any place I had ever been. Even the people I knew who claimed to possess the gift never explained how it worked. They simply opened their mouths, spoke the words, and concluded with, "Thus saith the Lord." I decided to wait.

In the meantime, a curious phenomenon began to occur. The word around the coffeehouse was that God was about to move in a major way in our midst. The last days were here, the Antichrist was on the move, and Jesus was due to arrive any day. We were about to see signs and wonders unlike anything the church had ever experienced before, and the Lost Coin was going to be the epicenter of it all.

That's right. All the things you have read about in the book of Revelation were about to issue forth from our little coffeehouse.

I must admit, as I write these words, it is hard for me to believe we could not see the conceit in all of this. Not in the fact that God might move in a remarkable way or even that he would cause signs and wonders to occur prior to the return of Christ. It is the ego-centricity of it all that amazes me. I am stunned by our assumption that our little group was the focal point—or that I might have a ministry which eclipsed one of the greatest prophets in the Bible. I can only tell you that as I was going through it, it seemed perfectly reasonable.

On the other hand, I do understand how my reasoning worked. It was not because I was convinced I was anything great but just the opposite. I knew I was a nobody and that God often worked through such people. My Bible told me God came to stutterers like

Moses, cowards like Gideon, teenagers like David, and blue-collar types like Simon Peter. He often used the unlikely and sometimes commanded the unreasonable. I could think of no one more unlikely and few things more unreasonable. It sounded like the essence of faith to me.

But I still faced a dilemma. How could I know it was God speaking to me? What should I say? I was not hearing voices. In fact, I couldn't hear anything when I prayed beyond my own confused thoughts. If only God could give me some sort of signal to let me know when he was in the neighborhood.

It came in the form of a tremor. Think of it as a spasm. Sometimes it was accompanied by a guttural noise, sort of like a case of spiritual Tourette's syndrome.

In the medieval world the monks prayed for the stigmata, visible marks on their hands, feet, and side to match the wounds of Christ. They considered them a special blessing and a sign that they had been set apart by God. These spasms were my stigmata. It started when I prayed. After a while it happened even when I wasn't praying. I often took it as a sign God was behind whatever I happened to be doing at the time. For example, I was looking over the books for sale at a Bible study and saw an interesting volume. I picked it up and there it was—uncontrollable shaking. I took it as a sign the Holy Spirit wanted me to buy the book.

I was encouraged by this strange experience, taking it as confirmation that God was indeed using me in a remarkable way. But I still wasn't getting any messages. I was eager to speak for God. I just didn't know what to say. I was getting a little impatient, wondering when the Holy Spirit was going to use me. Apparently, I wasn't the only one, because one night Dave spoke to me about it.

"The Lord wants you to speak, brother." There was sternness in his voice, the tone a parent might use toward a child who has been told to do something more than once and has stubbornly refused. I felt a stab of panic. Could I have missed the signals?

I paused and searched my thoughts again. Still no voices. I had no clear sense of what God might want to say through me. Yet Dave said God was waiting for me to speak.

I pictured him standing with his arms folded and his feet tapping.

The heavy silence seemed to say, "Well?"

I did the only thing I could think of to do.

I started to speak. I spoke off the top of my head, without planning and without reflection. Once I got started the words came tumbling out, like water going over a waterfall. They concerned Frank, an evangelist who led a large Friday night worship meeting at a nearby church. I often attended Frank's meetings. Frank, I heard myself say, was filled with pride. The Lord wanted him to step down and wanted Alex, his second-in-command, to take his place. There was a long silence when I finished. Who knew?

"Wow!" someone finally whispered.

We sat for several minutes looking at one another with amazement, trying to process my message. Then Dave spoke.

"Somebody's got to tell Frank."

I hadn't thought of that.

Frank was once part of a notorious motorcycle gang. He came to Christ after being shot in the head. Frank recovered when someone prayed for him. Sometime later Frank had an encounter with God that changed his life. He made his living as a barber now, but his real calling was as an evangelist. Every Friday night he preached to hundreds of young people.

Who would tell Frank that God wanted him to step down? I certainly didn't envy that person his job.

I realized Dave was staring at me. With a wry smile he said, "Well, brother, the Lord gave the prophecy through you." Something about the situation reminded me of the old children's story of the mice who debated about who was to place the bell around the cat's neck.

I went home and agonized over what to do next. Yes, I wanted to be a prophet, but I had no desire to say anything to Frank. How did I know the message was from God? On the other hand, it certainly wasn't something I had considered prior to that night. Frank didn't seem to be full of pride to me. Why would I have said such a thing if it hadn't come from the Lord? Perhaps this was a test. After all, how would I ever speak before kings and rulers if I was too afraid to confront a local preacher? There was only one thing for me to do. I had to talk to Frank. If God called me to be a prophet, I needed to be a prophet. Somehow I managed to obtain his phone number. It was easier than trying to confront him face to face. My hands trembled as I dialed, hoping with all my might that he was unavailable. At least I could say I tried.

To my horror, Frank's voice came on the line.

"Uh, Frank?"

"Yeah?"

"Uh, my name is John. You don't know me, but I have a message from the Lord for you." My voice was barely audible.

There was a long pause.

I went on, wishing it would end soon. "Well, um, the Lord says you're full of pride, and he wants you to step down and let Alex take over."

Frank blew up.

"I know about you people and what you've been doing," he thundered. "I've been cleaning up the mess you've been making all week. If you don't stop, I'm going to see to it that you are banned from every fellowship in the Detroit area."

I was terrified.

"I'm sorry," I said. "I'm just trying to obey God."

He calmed down.

"Look," he said, "you sound like a sincere guy. Why don't you come before the meeting next Friday, and I'll show you some things from the Bible about the gift of prophecy."

Relieved, I agreed to meet him.

On Friday, he sat down with me and turned to several passages of Scripture. He explained the purpose of biblical prophecy, saying it was to build up God's people and that there were certain marks that validated a prophet's ministry. It wasn't unusual phenomena or even miracles that proved a prophet's word was the word of the Lord but consistency with what God had already said in Scripture. God, Frank told me, never contradicts himself. What is more, he went on, biblical prophecy was always 100 percent accurate. This disturbed me because I knew some of the prophecies uttered by our little group had not come to pass. We usually attributed it to lack of faith on the part of those who heard. Now I questioned whether we were listening to God at all. Finally, Frank began to talk about his own ministry.

"Do you think what I do is glamorous?" he asked.

The question was rhetorical, but the answer was yes. It did seem glamorous to me. I considered people like Frank to be the celebrities of the church. Their ministries were high profile. We all looked up to them and admired what they did. To be honest, one of the reasons I was attracted to the gift of prophecy was because I wanted to be up front. I wanted people to listen to me.

"It may look glamorous," he went on, "but it's not. If I had my way, I'd rather be back on the street sticking a needle in my vein! But do you know why I don't go back? Because every week hundreds of kids like you show up who need to know Jesus Christ. That's why I do what I do."

What I heard sobered me. So this was what ministry was all about. It wasn't about me and my gifts. It was about serving others and speaking the truth. It was about glorifying Christ and building up his church. Frank prayed with me and went out to preach the message for the evening.

Next to my conversion, that meeting was the most important turning point in my spiritual life. It forced me to question the validity of my faith. Had I been wrong about everything? If I was mistaken about this message I thought came from God, might not everything I believed about Jesus be wrong? This question, in turn, forced me to reevaluate the basis for my faith. What, after all, had attracted me to Christ in the first place? Hadn't it been my reading of the Scriptures? But now the Bible was less important to me than the immediacy of prophecy.

It occurred to me that if the Bible is truly God's Word, as it claimed to be, then what it said was as immediate as if God spoke audibly. What is more, it was the only word I could be sure was 100 percent accurate. I determined from that point on to base my faith on the truth of Scripture and to judge my experiences by it rather than the other way around. I began to read the Bible regularly. The tremors died down and our little band of prophets eventually dissolved. I concluded I did not, in fact, have the gift of prophecy, but I did want to preach. Not for the glamour of it but for the sake of those who needed to hear the truth of Scripture. I delivered my first sermon at the Lost Coin and have been preaching ever since.

And Frank? He eventually stepped out of his role as evangelist, and Alex took over.

CHAPTER 13

At Calvary

Calvary was the second Baptist church I attended and the largest church I'd ever seen. A full house at the Lost Coin didn't even fill the first row at Calvary. With its plush seats, large stage, and giant choir, it reminded me of a movie theater more than a church. This was ironic, since the folks at Calvary were dead set against the theater. Anyone who wanted to be a member promised not to go to the movies or engage in other "worldly" entertainment.

There were other expectations as well. At Calvary we couldn't drink, dance, or smoke. We were expected to shun playing cards, although the spiritual threat they posed was not clear to me.

Calvary was famous for Pastor Jeff, its white-suited, trumpet-playing minister of music. He opened the service each Sunday by welcoming the congregation with his mellifluous radio voice and telling us how good we looked. He led congregational singing with a sharp snap of his fingers and broad sweeping gestures that seemed to have no correlation to the beat of the music. Once a year he was called upon to fill the pulpit in the senior pastor's absence, always preaching what sounded to me like the same sermon. The same was true of the vocal solos he sometimes sang in a deep warbling bass which made every melody line sound identical to my untrained ear.

This was not the case when it came to his trumpet. A virtuoso on the horn, he could have made a living playing in a big band. His trademark flourish was an earsplitting crescendo that brought his trumpet solos to a finish worthy of Doc Severenson, the band leader on the *Tonight Show*. At Thanksgiving and Christmas the church staged giant choral productions featuring Christian recording artists. They reminded me of the kind of thing one might find in a nightclub or in Las Vegas, but without the dancing girls. I was impressed by the church. I liked the red carpet and the way the gentle *thup* echoed throughout the sanctuary as the upholstered theater seats snapped to attention behind us when we rose to sing hymns. I liked the way the women wore dresses and the men in their business suits carried Bibles. I wanted to be like them.

One of the church's favorite hymns was "At Calvary." The chorus went, "Mercy there was great and grace was free. Pardon there was multiplied to me. There my burdened soul found liberty, at Calvary." The first time I heard it, I thought they were singing about the church. It sounded conceited to me until I realized the song was about the place where Jesus died.

The sermons I heard at Calvary differed from the preaching at Glad Tidings. Pastor Adams, the senior pastor, was a man noted for his ability to memorize the Bible. He did not flush red or stomp his feet when he preached. He did not shout glory and clap his hands. He merely stood at the pulpit and talked. What he lacked in energy, he made up in content. His tendency to quote long passages of Scripture prompted some in the church to refer to him as "the walking Bible." The quotations came in sudden bursts and were executed with lightning speed. The words ran together in a way that made it hard to distinguish one from another. He could have said anything and we probably wouldn't have noticed.

Whenever he spoke of wicked Queen Jezebel, which was fairly often, he spat her name syllable by syllable, as if his righteous tongue could hardly bear to form the sound. He noted King Solomon's lament that he could find one upright man among a thousand, but no upright woman among them all. "No wonder," he complained, "look at the kind of women Solomon associated with."

We got the impression that the world was filled with godless and profane men and weak-willed women who needed to come forward during the altar call. Hearing about their plight made us feel glad we weren't one of them. At the conclusion of each message, the organ played and the congregation sang "Just As I Am." The pastor warned us each stanza might be the last, unless someone came forward. We prayed fervently for the unsaved to see the light and craned our necks to catch a glimpse of them as they stepped nervously down the aisle. When they did, we rejoiced with the hosts of heaven. We rejoiced too when they did not, secretly relieved that the service would not be prolonged by additional stanzas.

Calvary operated its own bookstore, offering a wide selection of the pastor's sermons for sale, all neatly bound so the congregation could study his messages at home. Donna, the college friend who first invited me to the church, gave me a copy of his series on the book of Revelation. Donna and I met in the Baptist Student Union at the community college we both attended. She was praying for Jack, the campus minister, to ask her out. Instead, I asked her out on a date. She told me later she grumbled to the Lord about it.

"Lord," she complained, "you must have misunderstood. I said 'Jack,' not 'John.'"

Meg, Donna's mother, was also disappointed when I showed up on her doorstep. After Donna and I dated a few times, Meg abruptly announced, "If you ever marry John, I will have a nervous breakdown."

Undeterred, I turned to the Scriptures for comfort, randomly opening the Bible to Genesis 29:18: "Jacob was in love with Rachel and said, 'I'll work for you seven years in return for your younger daughter Rachel.'" I took it as prophetic. I decided it must be a sign from God, urging me to pursue the relationship. I read further, hoping the passage revealed a biblical strategy for winning Donna's heart and changing her mother's disposition toward me. When I learned of the great lengths Jacob went to in order to appease Esau, I concluded God was telling me to embark on a whirlwind campaign of ingratiation. The strategy was to overwhelm them both with my love and attention. Over the next weeks I left notes on Donna's car, stopped by her house unexpectedly, and did favors for her parents. It never occurred to me how desperate this must have looked.

Meanwhile I wrestled with Calvary's theology. The folks at Calvary were the sort of Christians I was told did not possess the Holy Spirit, or at least possessed less of him than my "Spirit filled" friends. Their knowledge of Christ was supposed to be mere head knowledge and their lives devoid of spiritual power. Yet, if anything, they were more stable in their faith than many of the Christians I knew. They took their Bibles to church and shared the faith with their neighbors. When friends and family members got sick, they asked God to heal them, just like we did.

While the people at Calvary did not believe miraculous gifts like prophecy were commonplace, they too often acted as if God spoke to them directly. They made important decisions or shared their faith with people because they felt "led of the Lord" to do so. Donna claimed God worked small miracles in response to her prayers, like helping her find a good parking spot.

Although my experience with prophecy at the Lost Coin raised serious questions about the ministry of the Holy Spirit, doubts about speaking in tongues had already been growing for some time. I often spoke in tongues but wondered how I could be sure that what I was experiencing is what the Bible describes. I assumed they were identical but knew of no way to test this. It bothered me that I could turn the phenomenon on and off like water in a faucet. I didn't feel any closer to God when I spoke in tongues. I knew theologians sometimes spoke of tongues as an "ecstatic utterance," but I felt no ecstasy when I exercised the gift. If anything, I found the experience a little boring. I believed God still performed miracles, but I had never actually seen one take place. My attempts to invoke God's power to heal produced no results as far as I could tell.

If the things I experienced did not originate with God's Spirit, then what was their true source? In his preaching, the pastor at Calvary referred to "tongues speaking" Christians with the same contemptuous tone he reserved for heretics, hippies, and godless Queen Jezebel. What they attributed to the Holy Spirit, he attributed to Satan and self-deception.

This kind of talk made me equally nervous. Jesus condemned the Pharisees for making a similar suggestion about the miracles he performed. He warned his detractors that anyone who speaks against the Holy Spirit will not be forgiven, either in this age or the age to come (Matt. 12:32). I respected the pastor's learning but feared I might be on the verge of blaspheming the Holy Spirit.

Some of my Pentecostal friends expressed concern when they noticed me dividing my time between Glad Tidings and Calvary. Did I really need to go out with a Baptist, they wondered? Wasn't there a nice girl in our church that I could date? One of them even suggested I was involved in a cult. They wondered how I could worship in a spiritually dead church.

But I liked the change in worship style. It was a relief not to feel pressured to lift my hands and say "hallelujah" during worship. The sermons were more substantial, with a stronger focus on the biblical text.

Ironically, as I moved away from Pentecostal theology and practice, Donna and her mother were being drawn to it. Meg asked the church's bookstore to order titles that spoke favorably of miracles and miraculous gifts. These books weren't approved by Calvary's pastor and were kept off the shelves. They were sold "under the counter" like contraband to those who knew who to ask.

When Meg unexpectedly lost her hearing, the subject of divine healing became more than a matter of intellectual curiosity. Suddenly it was personal. Donna and her mother prayed about it and were both convinced the Lord would soon heal Meg's deafness. I, on the other hand, felt skeptical. I didn't question God's ability to heal in a miraculous way so much as his willingness to do so. My Pentecostal friends talked about miracles as if they were everyday occurrences, but I was hard pressed to find one that looked authentic. It was always a case of someone who knew someone who heard from someone who had witnessed a miracle. Direct proof was hard to find.

Meg was excited to learn the Happy Hunters, a couple widely known for their healing ministry, planned to hold a healing service in our area. She waited anxiously in a long line until it was her turn to experience the touch of their anointed hands. Those who were prayed for invariably collapsed as soon as they were touched by the happy couple, presumably under the powerful influence of the Holy Spirit. When her turn came, one of the Hunters muttered a brief prayer and tapped her on the head.

Nothing happened.

He tried again. This time he placed his palm on her forehead and gave it a forceful shove. Meg glared at the faith healer and refused to go down. She turned to her husband and with a note of indignation declared, "He's trying to push me over."

The disappointment Meg felt did not shake her conviction that God planned to heal her. But the incident only served to amplify my doubts. It all came to a head when I attended a healing service with Donna and her mother featuring Kathryn Kuhlman. Although she is relatively unknown today, many Pentecostals considered Kuhlman to be a revivalist equal to Billy Graham and a healer on a par with Oral Roberts. Kuhlman was as much a celebrity as she was a healer, appearing on television with Johnny Carson, Merv Griffin, and Mike Douglas. This was the big time and as good an opportunity as any for God to deliver on his promise to Donna and her mother.

Kuhlman's miracle service, held at the fieldhouse on the campus of the University of Michigan, began with music. As we sang about miracles and God's power to heal, I scanned the floor from our place high in the bleachers. With its army of wheelchairs and row upon row of beds filled with the sick and paralyzed, it looked as if the university's hospital had been emptied for the event. Kuhlman paced back and forth across the stage, her white gown billowing and her arms raised as if in blessing. She delivered her message in a kind of spiritual stream of consciousness punctuated by breathy whispers, drawn-out syllables, and elongated vowels.

I found the sermon hard to follow, perhaps because I was nervous about the outcome. My persistent doubt irritated Donna. She said it might have been better if I hadn't come. Unable to hear the proceedings, her mother watched the crowd anxiously, as if hoping to spot the location of the Holy Spirit in the auditorium.

I tried to concentrate on Kuhlman's message. She assured us that the power to heal did not reside with her. She did not claim to control God's power and could not predict how the Holy Spirit might move. She said God could not be blamed if someone wasn't healed. His power was unlimited. She could not be blamed either, since the power did not belong to her. The fault, as far as I could tell, was ours alone, should healing fail to occur.

Suddenly Kuhlman announced the Holy Spirit was on the move. I looked eagerly at Meg to see if anything had happened yet. There was no change, so I turned my attention to the sea of hospital beds that covered the floor. Nothing there either. Shouts of praise erupted in the bleachers across the way as people started making their way down to the stage to testify about the miracles they were experiencing. God, we were told, was busy healing neck pain and arthritis. No one stirred among the beds. I hadn't seen anyone get up from their wheelchair.

Recalling the accounts of healing in the Gospels, I questioned whether the experience of New Testament believers had been anything like this. Matthew 4:23 said that Jesus went throughout Galilee "healing every disease and sickness among the people." On another occasion it says he healed all who were brought to him (Matt. 8:16). When he moved among the crowds, the paralyzed took up their mats and walked, seizures disappeared, the blind saw, and the deaf heard. From my vantage point there in the bleachers, it seemed the Holy Spirit had confined his activity to the bleachers, shunning the hospital beds and wheelchairs.

The long service finally came to an end and Meg was still deaf, no better than when we arrived. As we stepped down from the bleachers, I glanced one last time at the broken bodies massed on the floor below. Watching as family members and friends wheeled them out of the auditorium, returning them to their hospitals, nursing homes, and sick rooms, I wondered what they thought of Kuhlman's apologetic a few minutes earlier? If she was not responsible and God could not be blamed, who was left? Did they blame themselves for not returning home whole?

I wondered who Donna and her mother blamed. They came confident in God's ability to heal and convinced he had promised them a healing. They could not be accused of having too little faith.

I rode home in silence, worried they might blame me. Did my doubt keep the Holy Spirit from working?

That night I decided not to go back to the Lost Coin. I stopped attending Glad Tidings and eventually became a member of Calvary. When the deacons questioned me about my views on the Holy Spirit, I said I was reluctant to define his ministry in terms of what he would not do. The Holy Spirit, if he chose, was still able to perform miracles. He could, if he wished, cause someone to speak in a tongue that they had not learned if it helped the spread of the gospel.

"But of course God wouldn't need to do that," one of the deacons explained. Flashing the kind of patronizing smile a parent might give to a well-meaning child who has just said something foolish, he explained, "That's why we send missionaries to language school."

I was considering other changes as well. Weary of my courses as a psychology major, I decided to transfer to a Bible college. It was a difficult decision to make. My father was unlikely to support such a plan, and I didn't know how to pay for the school's room and board. Donna and her family encouraged me to apply to the Moody Bible Institute in Chicago. I'd never heard of the school. But if they thought well of it, perhaps they would think the same of me if I attended.

I was taken aback by the personal details required by the school's application. It asked whether I had ever used alcohol, tobacco, or drugs and about a number of other intimate details about my life that I didn't even want my parents to know. After checking off all the items that applied, I was expected to write a statement promising I would never do such things again.

This put me in a difficult position. To make such a statement seemed boastful to me. I thought of Simon Peter's bold promise to follow Christ to the death and his subsequent betrayal. I certainly didn't want to make a similar mistake. So I checked off all the sins I had committed and wrote a long disclaimer. While I couldn't promise for certain I would never do such things again, I did not intend to go back to my old life.

Meanwhile, God's plan for my life was coming together nicely. I could see my whole future laid out before me. I would graduate from Moody Bible Institute, marry Donna, and go into the ministry. Someday I would pastor a big church with red carpet and plush theater seats. It couldn't have been clearer if it had come down from heaven in writing. I considered it a promise from God, the way Donna and Meg believed God promised to work a miracle of healing.

Donna went away to college in Indiana and broke up with me a few months later. I suppose I should have seen it coming when the letter from Moody Bible Institute arrived, saying they had rejected my application. If not then, I should have seen the writing on the wall the weekend I visited her at college. She asked me to stay out of sight while she said goodbye to one of the fellows who was leaving on a class retreat. The signals were as plain as day, but I still felt blindsided when she came home for Christmas break and told me she didn't want to date me anymore. It's hard to let go of your dreams, especially when you think they have been sanctioned by God.

I see now that what I took to be a promise was at best wishful thinking. At worst it was a form of presumption. I am not so different from my friends who believed miraculous gifts are everyday occurrences. Some had a magical view of God, in which prayer functioned like an incantation. Those who possessed that mysterious quality of faith and said the right words could control the hand of God. They believed that if you prayed in faith, God had no choice. He had to grant your request. Others used the lack of faith to tie God's hands. Or at least to provide him with an excuse when he did not answer as expected. God, they asserted, is fully able and willing to answer every prayer and heal every disease. He would like to do more for us, but cannot. It is not his fault. To me this sounded more like an attempt to provide God with an alibi.

When I left my Pentecostal roots behind, I discovered my non-Pentecostal friends were equally prone to presumption, but in a different vein. Instead of being presumptuous about what God would do for them, they were more inclined to make assumptions about what God would not do. Theologically, I am a cessationist, one who believes the miraculous gifts primarily served as validating marks of the apostles' ministry and are no longer the norm for today. But I am still uncomfortable with a theology that defines the ministry of the Holy Spirit primarily in terms of what he will not do. To do so is as presumptuous as believing God must heal whenever I ask. If my Pentecostal friends expect too much from God, I fear I expect too little.

Despite their significant differences in theology, both camps share a common temptation. Each wants to control God. He, of course, will not permit it. God makes his own plans and often carries them out in ways that are unfathomable to us. "Many are the plans in a human heart," Proverbs 19:21 declares, "but it is the Lord's purpose that prevails."

The year after Donna and I stopped dating, a friend at Calvary introduced me to Jane, the woman who became the love of my life and the mother of my two children. At the time, neither of us realized the significance of the moment. The meeting that profoundly shaped the rest of my life came without fanfare. There was no heavenly vision and no voice from above. Jane didn't like the way I looked. I barely noticed her. I suppose some might say it was a miracle we ever got together.

Meg eventually did regain some of her hearing, though not through the ministry of some faith healer. Rather, her "healing" came as a result of a surgical procedure. Was that a miracle too? Most would probably say no. But if the cure comes by the hand of the physician, is it any less the power of God that works healing? I doubt Meg thought so.

I finally did end up at the Moody Bible Institute, but not as a student. The school that rejected my application eventually hired me as a professor. The opportunity came unexpectedly, after years of praying without much hope that such a thing would really come to pass. I submitted my resume more than once, only to receive a polite reply each time informing me there were no openings. I even taught part time on the main campus for a semester, driving four hours each way to teach two students, neither of whom was especially interested in my class. I prayed the administration would take notice of me and offer me a full-time position. But when I mentioned my desire to the dean, his reply was blunt.

"Don't get your hopes up," he said. "We don't have much turnover among the faculty."

I went back to my office and complained to God.

"Lord," I said, "you were supposed to open a door for me here." I immediately repented, certain that my request was presumptuous.

As it turns out, the dean and I were both wrong.

CHAPTER 14

Family Man

I pulled the covers over my head at the sound of footsteps as they echoed in the hall. Stiff with fear, I held my breath and waited for the scream I knew would soon follow. The weekend had arrived and *The Mummy* was on the loose again. Or was it *The Mummy's Ghost*? Creatures like Frankenstein's Monster and the Creature from the Black Lagoon went on the prowl every Friday night when my parents watched *Shock Theater*, a late-night television program that featured old horror films. I wasn't permitted to watch. The program aired late at night and my parents were concerned the show might give me nightmares. I suppose they were right. Still, I doubt the black-and-white images that flickered on the screen could have been more terrifying than those conjured by my imagination as I lay in the darkness of my bedroom and listened to the dialog.

The host began each program by exhorting viewers to lock the doors and turn out the lights. Had I not been so terrified by the funereal sound of his voice, which alone was enough to make me pull the covers up over my head, I would have done just the opposite. But the prospect of rising from my bed to make my way across the dark room was too daunting a challenge. Who knows what might happen in the transit between the bed and the light switch on the opposite wall?

During the day my room looked like any ordinary boy's bedroom, an untidy heap of clothes, toys, and other odds and ends. But at night this otherwise-friendly territory took on an entirely different aspect, transforming these once familiar mounds of childhood debris into a strange and menacing landscape. Suddenly I found myself surrounded by hideous forms, while the open door of the closet at the foot of my bed grew large, a black portal prepared to release unimagined horrors into the world.

Occasionally I contemplated making a dash for the door and racing down the hall into the living room, where my father slumped on my mother's shoulder dozing as she absently drank her beer and watched the gothic tale unfolding on the screen before her. But it was safer to stay in my bed clinging to the sheets and endure the relentless shuffle of whatever happened to be the creature of the evening than to brave the terrors of the dark. Besides, I knew the real horror began after the program ended, when my mother woke my father from his alcohol-induced slumber and the two of them began to fight.

I grew up watching *Leave It to Beaver*, *Donna Reed*, and *Father Knows Best*, television programs that taught me what family life was supposed to be like. Mom was supposed to wear a dress and bake cookies. Dad's job was to dispense wise advice with patience. The house was supposed to be clean, the arguments polite, and every family crisis was to be neatly resolved with group laughter in thirty minutes or less. On nights like the one when my mother broke a beer bottle over my father's head as he slept and my father threatened to burn down the house with a kerosene lantern, it dawned on me that I didn't live in such a family.

I didn't acquire a vocabulary to explain our brand of family life until I reached my thirties. That was when I discovered I grew up in a "dysfunctional" home, a term that by now has become as cliched as television's vision of family life in the '50s and '60s. Some shows emphasize the "fun" in dysfunctional, trivializing the chaos that defines what is considered normal in such families, while others cast it in the gothic colors of a horror film. For me, growing up in a dysfunctional family was a little of both, part situation comedy and part *Shock Theater*.

When I was in junior high school my mother suffered a nervous breakdown. Already a late riser who typically didn't wake up until noon, she now stayed in bed for days at a time. When she left her room, which was rare, she drifted through the house like a ghost.

Dirty dishes collected in the sink and unwashed clothes piled up to mountainous proportions. My father claimed it was only the flu, but I didn't believe it. Still, we went about our daily affairs trying to pretend everything was normal.

At some point in her downward spiral, she dragged herself out of bed, put on makeup and a nice dress, and sat sullenly in the car as my father drove her to a psychiatrist. The therapist listened as she described the black depression that engulfed her. When she stated her conviction that we were better off without her, he interrupted with a question.

"Mrs. Koessler, do you know where babies come from?"

She swore at him, stormed out of the office, and went back to bed.

A few days later I came home from school and found her seated in her usual spot on the couch. Wild eyed, she explained she planned to divorce my father.

"You need to decide who you want to live with," she demanded.

I questioned the seriousness of her intention, not to mention the reasonableness of her plan. Without a driver's license or job, she couldn't support herself, let alone us. Hoping to keep her from doing anything rash, I tried to put her off.

"I don't want to make a choice," I said. "I want the two of you to stay together."

"You have to decide," she insisted. "Is it going to be with him or with me?"

"Then I won't live with either of you," I said. I hoped my reasoning might shock her into a different course of action, but it didn't work. She continued to demand that I pick one of them. I decided to base my choice on pragmatic grounds.

"All right," I said. "I choose Dad. He's the one with the job and the car."

She looked as if I had slapped her. But the emotional blow of my words failed to bring her to her senses. If anything, it drove her farther into her cave of despondency. The manic gleam in her eye disappeared, replaced now by a dark cloud. She reached the low point in her descent the night she tried to take her life with one of my father's razor blades, spattering the mirror and the sink with her torment.

This went on for several weeks. Then suddenly, inexplicably, it ended. Mother got out of bed on a Sunday morning and made breakfast. She set the table with china and silverware and sat with us to eat, something she never did even when she was in her right mind. I hardly knew what to think. The day before, she was so overwhelmed with despair she couldn't dress herself, and now she was seated at the table, clothed and in her right mind. The next Sunday she made breakfast again. And the Sunday after that. I spent each meal in wide-eyed amazement, afraid to do or say anything that might break the spell.

As my mother began to emerge from her cave of despair, my father descended into his own heart of darkness. Always a heavy drinker on the weekends, he now exhibited the signs I later learned marked him as an alcoholic. Weekend binges bled over into the weekdays. He sometimes stopped at the bar while on errands to the cleaners or the drugstore. After my mother's death, his problem grew worse. He drank vodka by the half gallon and started taking "vacation days" during the week. He drank so much he seemed to bleed alcohol, the sour smell of it coming from his pores like sweat.

I listened for his footsteps in the hall late at night and the erratic thump as he rebounded from wall to wall on his stumbling path to bed. On some nights I awoke to a loud crash as he missed his target and collapsed on the floor at the foot of my bed. Because he was too heavy for me to lift, I helped him crawl to his own room next door. Other nights he didn't come home at all.

I was not dismayed to learn that what we considered normal was actually dysfunctional. To the contrary, this realization came as something of a relief to me. It helped me understand the strange mixture of bedlam and boredom that characterized our home and showed me our problems were not as unique as I once thought.

I was further relieved when I discovered the Bible's remarkable assortment of family portraits, a painful array of flawed relationships that made my family look practically healthy by comparison. I read about the jealousy of Adam's son Cain, which motivated him to murder his brother, Abel (Gen. 4:8). It surprised me to learn that Noah, a man so righteous he was chosen to preserve the human race, got drunk (Gen. 9:21). So did Lot, and as a result his daughters committed incest with him (Gen. 19:30–38).

Parental favoritism caused Abraham's grandsons Jacob and Esau to spend most of their lives feuding with one another. Jacob's two wives bartered with each other for the right to have relations with him (Gen. 30:14–16). Jacob followed his parents' example of favoritism and so embittered his own children that they sold their brother Joseph into slavery (Gen. 37:3–28). Jacob's son Judah slept with his daughter-in-law when she disguised herself as a prostitute (Gen. 38:15–16). This was just the first book of the Bible!

David, a man after God's own heart, committed adultery and murder and was guilty of parental neglect (2 Sam. 12:9–12; 1 Kings 1:5–6). Because of this, his family eventually disintegrated in a tragic sequence of events including rape, incest, and murder. Even Jesus' family had its problems. Jesus was ridiculed by his brothers and was called mad by his extended family (Mark 3:21). The Bible's list of dysfunctional families, I found, was a long and sordid one, suggesting family life, even among the saints, can be messy.

The Scriptures helped me to see that my family background was no accident. God's redeeming work carried me through my painful past and guided me into a better future (Jer. 29:11; Rom. 8:28). When I look beyond the pain of my parents' alcoholism and depression, I can trace the marks of God's hand working to mark the path that led to a relationship with him.

Like Joseph, who was verbally and physically abused by his brothers and then sold into slavery, every circumstance in my life was subordinated to a larger purpose. Joseph could tell his brothers, "You intended to harm me, but God intended it for good to accomplish what is now being done, the saving of many lives" (Gen. 50:20). If this could be said of intentional evil, it must be just as true of the unintentional harm inflicted by my parents.

So why, even after I moved out on my own, did I still wake up in a panic in the middle of the night, listening anxiously to the sounds of the house as it shifted on its foundation? When the neighbors upstairs fought, I pulled the covers over my head and plugged my ears, as if I were still a child in my parents' house. There were moments of sudden despair, when a black fog settled over my soul for no apparent reason. This was coupled with seasons of self-doubt, when I magnified every failure and considered any success an accident. I felt insecure about my lovers and friends, like the unwelcome guest who knows his presence is tolerated only for the sake of politeness.

After my father died of alcoholism, I found some help by spending time in counseling and group therapy. But the chief instruments God used to bring about healing were my wife and children.

My wife, Jane, entered my life in an unexpected moment of grace, when she decided to give me a second chance after our initial meeting and attended a Bible study I led. She flashed a radiant smile from across the room and I felt as if all my secrets were laid bare before her. I blushed and looked away, then felt compelled to look again. After twenty-six years of marriage her smile still has the power to leave me dumbfounded.

One of Jane's greatest gifts is her capacity to find God in the small things of the day. She taught me to see the routine as a means of grace. In the early days of my walk with Christ, I was told, "Expect great things from God; attempt great things for God." Jane showed me the importance of investing in the unremarkable. When I worried that I wasn't ambitious enough, she quoted 1 Thessalonians 4:11 – 12 to me: "Make it your ambition to lead a quiet life, to mind your own business and to work with your hands, just as we told you, so that your daily life may win the respect of outsiders and so that you will not be dependent on anybody."

A few months after our wedding, she and I attended the wedding of a college friend who asked me to be one of his groomsmen. When the groom introduced me at the reception, I was shocked to hear my normally reticent wife erupt in a raucous cheer. A few minutes later, one of the bridesmaids confronted me.

"I just want to know who you are that you should get such a round of applause," she asked.

With a sheepish smile, I pointed to Jane. "It wasn't everybody," I said. "It was just my wife."

The woman scowled. "She must really love you to be married to you and still cheer like that."

More than a quarter of a century later, Jane is still cheering. Passionate in her devotion, she is the one person I can be sure will always tell me the truth. "You're not going to like this," she will say, "but I'm going to tell you anyway."

Jane was hit by a car in her freshman year of high school and spent several months in a cast. About the time she was fully mended, her father was diagnosed with cancer and died a short time later. She was a new believer, only a few months old in the Lord. These two events provided a context that grounded her faith in realism. They also taught her to depend upon God.

For Jane the cost of following Christ could be measured in the miles that separated her from the family she loved. I felt called to ministry early in my Christian experience. Jane and I discussed the implications of this when we dated. Such a call meant she must leave her family behind and move with me, first to the hills of Pennsylvania and then to the plains of central Illinois. She felt the weight of the cross bear down upon her with fresh weight each time we said goodbye to her mother after our visits home. No doubt following Christ has cost others more. Still, such knowledge is cold comfort when the time comes to love Christ more than one's mother or father. She has never complained about the sacrifice, even though what has been gain for me has mostly meant loss for her.

God used Jane's habit of sanctifying the commonplace to introduce a quiet rhythm where there once was chaos in my life. Her encouragement has given me permission to succeed, and her constant love allows me the freedom to fail. She is my best friend and my greatest fan.

Next to my wife, the two people who have influenced my view of God the most have been my sons, Drew and Jarred. Like most of the important lessons of life, this happened almost incidentally. They did not set out to be my teachers. When the nurse handed me my firstborn, a squirming bundle of life tightly wrapped in a blanket, I knew my life would never be the same again. Excited and terrified at the prospect of being parents, Jane and I brought his crib into our bedroom. We tuned our ears to hear the slightest rustle and coo. "So this is what it is like to be a father," I thought, wondering whether I would ever sleep again.

Fatherhood became a mirror that helped me to understand what it means to be a child of God. I saw in my love for my children a dim reflection of the Father's love for me. It startled me to discover how quickly my ear became attuned to the sound of their voices and how much pleasure we derived simply from being together. If I could find such joy in my own children, how much more must it be true of God in his disposition toward me?

I understood Jesus' words in Matthew 7:11 in a new light: "If you, then, though you are evil, know how to give good gifts to your children, how much more will your Father in heaven give good gifts to those who ask him!" I was amazed by my children's confidence in my ability to provide for their needs, solve their problems, and act as their champion—a trust that seemed to border on worship at times. Time and again they laid before me the shattered remains of their broken treasures, supremely confident in my ability to repair the damage. Fearless in their requests, my children were not ashamed to tell me their needs and were never afraid to express their desires. To them no request was outside the scope of my interest and no wish beyond my ability to grant. Even though this expectation modified somewhat as they grew into teenagers and began to recognize my limitations, they continued to take my love for granted, assuming I would not give them a stone if they asked for bread.

On weekends when I cut the grass, I watched my son Drew, bent over his little plastic mower, trying in earnest to match my stride. His younger brother, Jarred, slipped in front of me, barely tall enough to reach the mower's handle and too small to propel the mower by his own power. I pushed it for him, doubling the length of time needed to finish the job. When we were done Jarred rushed into the house, beamed up at his mother, and announced with obvious pride, "I helped Daddy cut the grass!"

Surely the things I do for God are just as trifling, my best work play and the pride I feel in my accomplishments merely childish bravado. Is it really possible that God feels the same joy in my collaboration with him that I experienced in the company of my two boys? Even more astonishing, the Bible promises a day is coming when I will receive praise from God for what I have done.

My field of interest, too, is often equally small. Like the child who prefers the box to the gift and weeps over the loss of some trinket, my ambitions must seem frivolous and my sorrows absurd when compared with God's true purpose for my life. Yet time and again he has granted me the desire of my heart in the hope that the experience of his goodness will impel my heart to respond to a higher call.

Having children of my own has helped me view my parents' behavior through a lens of grace. Recognizing my weaknesses has helped me to accept theirs. They bore their own scars and did not have the advantage of the grace I have been given. What is more, not every example they provided was bad. Despite their fighting, I never doubted my parents' love for each other. Seeing my mother welcome my father home each night with a long kiss taught me the importance of a loving touch. Noting that some of my favorite memories revolve around long walks and late-night conversations showed me that my children are as interested in simply being with me as they are in doing something with me. Many of the abilities and interests I now enjoy, such as my love for reading, passion for the truth, and appreciation of a neatly crafted phrase, are all part of their legacy to me.

Some time ago I spoke with a friend who also grew up in a dysfunctional home about the common sense of dread we both feel as the holidays approach. Time off in my home usually meant my parents drank. Sometimes the results were terrifying. At others the resulting chaos could be comical. When my brother and sister and I reminisce about our childhood, we often find ourselves laughing.

Perhaps this is only a defense mechanism. We laugh because the only alternative is crying.

But more often than not we laugh because the memories are genuinely pleasant. Like the time we got so caught up in the fervor of a Fourth of July celebration that we decided to have a parade. My sister got her baton. We grabbed the American flag from its holder on the porch and lined up along the sidewalk in front of our house. All that was missing was the marching band. That was when we remembered my father knew how to play the trumpet! When we asked him to join our parade, he said no. But we begged and pleaded until, amazingly, he consented. I still smile when I think of what it must have looked like to the neighbors as we marched around the block in single file, with my father bringing up the rear blowing a Sousa march on his trumpet.

Although I would prefer to live without emotional scars, they have taught me an invaluable truth. They have shown me that my actions will affect my children for years to come. There are no truly individual acts. This, of course, is the fundamental principle of community life reflected in the experience of the church. The behavior of one has implications for many: "If one part suffers, every part suffers with it; if one part is honored, every part rejoices with it" (1 Cor. 12:26).

What is true of the church in a spiritual sense is true of the family in a natural sense. Every choice I make has an impact on my wife and my children. It has been thirty years since my mother's death, and my father has been gone for eighteen, yet I feel the impact of their broken lives every day. There are nights when I am still haunted by the memories of years gone by. I do not always find it easy to sleep at night, when many of the bad things that happened in my home took place. I will sometimes wake at the slightest noise with my heart pounding, the sound of terrors long past reverberating in my memory like echoes from a distant canyon.

On one such night, I couldn't help but notice how the noise of the house shifting on its foundations sounded as if someone were walking down the hall toward our bedroom. The noise was familiar to me. So was the creeping sense of dread that accompanied it. A host of painful memories came to me in quick succession. I remembered the night my mother threatened to stab my father with a butcher knife, the night I walked into the bathroom and saw her blood spattered across the sink and the mirror, the time my father took his rifle from the closet and spent the night contemplating taking his own life.

Each memory brought with it a renewed sense of the fear and despair I experienced as a child. My wife, awakened by my tossing and turning, asked me what was wrong.

"I don't know," I said, and described the memories to her.

She didn't shrug them off or try to explain them away. Instead, she put her arms around me and gently spoke the words that calmed my fears and healed my broken soul more than any others I have heard.

"John," she whispered, "you don't live in that house anymore."

CHAPTER 15

Working for Jesus

I got the job that changed my life by accident. John, the manager of the Jack-in-the-Box restaurant near our house, thought he was hiring someone else and called me by mistake. "You sounded so surprised to get the job," he later told me, "I didn't have the heart to tell you it was a mistake."

I once asked John why he originally wanted to give the job to somebody else.

"It was your face," he said. "You looked so gloomy when you came in to fill out an application I didn't want to hire you."

The truth is, I didn't really want the job. Not at first.

Just graduated from high school, I couldn't decide what to do with the rest of my life. Poet, politician, and stand-up comedian all appealed to me as possible career paths. Eventually I combined all three and became a pastor. At that point, however, I felt compelled by necessity to seek more ordinary employment. My options were limited by both geography and experience. Without a car of my own, I was forced to find work within walking distance of our house. It was only the desire to have a vehicle of my own that initially compelled me to look for a job in the first place.

My resume was limited. My only previous job was scooping ice cream at a nearby Baskin Robbins. The work was hard at first. When I closed my eyes at night I saw open tubs of ice cream, their images permanently burned on the back of my retinas. When I fell asleep I dreamt about waiting on customers, leaving me with the feeling my work day was twice as long. The chief benefit of the job, other than its minimum-wage salary, was the opportunity to sample the ice cream we served. At night, after the store closed, I drank milk shakes and ate pizza. When I was done, I made myself a banana split for desert. I lost thirty pounds when I quit.

The only other employment to which I could lay claim was a one-day stint selling *Grit* newspapers door to door. I learned about the opportunity from an ad in the Superman comics I read. The ad itself consisted of a comic describing the adventures of Gritboy, whose financial woes are solved when he sells the weekly newspaper read by millions. In retrospect, I suppose the fact that the Detroit area already boasted two major daily papers and several community papers should have given me pause, but the ad said the paper practically sold itself. It promised I could make as much as twelve dollars a week, an unbelievable sum when compared to my ten-cent allowance. I could also earn fabulous prizes.

According to the folks at *Grit*, many millionaires and other famous people started down the path to success by selling their newspaper. This seemed like a good sign. I could tell they were on the level because the ad said I didn't need to send any money in advance and only paid for the newspapers I sold.

In a fever to begin making my fortune, I filled out the coupon and eagerly watched the mail. When the papers arrived, it bothered me a little that the front page featured a story about a space flight more than a week old. Everyone I knew saw it live on television. Still, the photograph was in color, a selling point.

As I contemplated the stack of papers that now looked impossibly large, it occurred to me I hadn't considered how I planned to find the people to buy them. My heart sank as I realized I needed to go door to door to peddle them. Apparently the people at *Grit* did not mean it literally when they said the paper sold itself.

I set off down the block with a bundle of papers under my arm, inordinately relieved when I rang the first few doorbells and no one answered. I felt the same way years later when evangelizing door to door with the church. It wasn't that I didn't want to tell others about Jesus. I was eager to share the Good News, as eager as I had been to peddle *Grit* to my neighbors. Something changed when I found myself face to face with a stranger. I grew bashful and inarticulate.

I finally came to a house where I heard footsteps behind the door. I panicked as it swung open and an unshaven fat man gruffly asked what I wanted. This was something I hadn't counted on; the papers were supposed to sell themselves.

"Uh, you wouldn't want to buy a newspaper, would you?" I mumbled in a barely audible voice. The man looked at me uncomprehendingly, as if I uttered the question in a foreign language. Encouraged by the pause, I added, "It's *Grit*," as if no other explanation were needed, and flashed the color photo on the front page.

His confused expression changed to one of scorn. With a dismissive grunt, he started to close the door.

"Nah," he said, "I already get two."

The rest of the block was the same. Either no one was home or they already subscribed to more than one paper. Until, at last, I came to a house where the *Grit* name lived up to its reputation. Reluctant at first, the middle-aged man with the Southern drawl brightened when I told him what I was selling.

"*Grit*?" he beamed. "Why we used to read that paper when I was a boy living on the farm."

Jubilant, I handed him a copy, only slightly damp from the sweat in my palms and slightly wrinkled from handling. He handed me thirty-five cents, twelve of which were mine to keep. If I sold ninety-nine more, the twelve dollars promised in the comic-book ad were mine.

I had sold only one copy of the paper by the time I reached the end of the block. Salesmanship was not my greatest strength. I would have to make my fortune some other way. I kept the twelve cents and returned the rest of the papers to *Grit* headquarters in Williamsport, Pennsylvania.

My sales ability didn't improve any by the time I graduated from high school. The day I walked into the Jack-in-the-Box restaurant to ask for a job, I might as well have been selling *Grit* newspapers.

"You wouldn't be hiring, would you?" I mumbled, barely looking at John. He handed me an application and I filled it out right there. Two days later I got the call.

It wasn't until I proved I could do the job that John finally told me it had all been a mistake. By then I was working the midnight shift, a seasoned veteran of the grill. Things had been a little shaky at first, the work overwhelming. Wednesday, the night I drained the boiling-hot fat from the fryers and carried it out to a large metal vat behind the dumpster, was the worst. That part of the job was dangerous; one slip and I would be covered with burns. The old grease sat in layers in the vat, each new coating leaving a cold grey memorial to the previous weeks' labor, the way the layers of sediment mark the age of the earth. Here and there a stray french fry lay entombed in the fat, like the remains of some prehistoric creature might be captured in amber and preserved for eternity.

The high point of every Wednesday came the moment I poured the new layer of fat on top of the old. Steam rose with a hiss and the vat churned like some witch's cauldron. It bubbled for a moment and then quickly settled. On the way back in the restaurant I always paused to watch the sky brightening in the east. I was proud of my ability to do the job.

John was one of the best employers I have ever had. Somehow John's way of asking those who worked for him to do difficult things made us feel like it was a privilege to comply. The work was important to him. Even more, John considered the humble task of making hamburgers a kind of art form. I could tell that working in the restaurant wasn't just a job for him. It was more of a calling. He had a gift for it.

"Someday I want to own my own restaurant," John once told me. "Not like this but the kind of place where I can wear a suit and a tie and mingle with the customers on the floor."

Customers were important to John. Sometimes late at night he dropped in unexpectedly and lined up with the other cars in the drive-through to see what the service was like. On one occasion he caught me slipping Christian tracts into the bags. He told me he appreciated my zeal, but it was against company policy. We talked about faith on numerous occasions. Each time, John showed a genuine interest, not only in what I believed but in why I believed it. He also took an interest in my personal life, setting up an appointment with his barber one weekend when he learned I was going out on an important date.

John was as much a shepherd as a manager. He showed me there is more to leadership than getting people to accomplish a task; it is a relationship. He believed our performance on the job was affected by our circumstances outside the workplace and often talked with us about our personal lives. He was the first one to model what it means to approach one's work as a vocation and showed me there is more to a job than work. The Jack-in-the-Box was not only the place where I felt Christ calling me to be his disciple; it was the place where I learned the first principles that contributed to my work ethic, a foundation I carried with me into the ministry.

John finally got the opportunity to manage a restaurant nice enough for him to wear a tie. I quit soon after and enrolled in college. I had a few brief stints working in a factory, got a job in a bookstore, and eventually ended up working the midnight shift again. This time I vacuumed rugs in a department store with an assortment of people who reminded me of the cast out of a Marx Brothers movie. Joe spent his early years digging coal in the mountains of Kentucky. Decades after he left the mine he still coughed up coal dust. Joe sometimes talked to me about what he had been taught in church as a young boy. In a strange mix of modernism and fundamentalism, he claimed the human race as we now know it was descended through Noah's sons, some of whom married apes. When I expressed my doubts about this, Joe assured me it was the gospel truth.

"It's in the Bible," he declared with a drawl. "I read it there ... somewhere. I just can't remember where."

Al was another coworker. Al grew up in Italy and referred to everyone as "Meester."

"Alo, Meester John," he declared in his thick accent whenever he saw me on the freight elevator. "Ow you tooday?" He greeted everyone the same way. Al's voice was so loud I could hear him talk as he vacuumed rugs two or three floors above me.

Harold was a premed student raised in the apostolic faith and annoyed by my habit of reading out of a pocket New Testament during lunch. Harold spent most of the lunch break harassing me, saying his mission was to try to make me swear. When I asked him why, he said it was because I claimed to be a Christian.

"You do what I'm supposed to do but don't," he said. "It bugs me. So I'm going to make you swear if it's the last thing I do."

Harold was intrigued by my desire to go into the ministry someday. He wondered how much money someone made in that line of work. I told him that I doubted I would make much.

"Why do it?" he asked.

"For the same reason you want to be a doctor," I replied, "to help people."

Harold's response was frank. "Oh, I want to be a doctor for the money." He smiled apologetically and then added, "Of course, I can't tell them that at my school. They would never have let me into the program."

After a few weeks I realized what bothered Harold was the way I sat apart from the rest of the crew during lunch. I did this partly as a "testimony," to show I was different. Harold's reaction made me realize it merely made me look aloof and unfriendly.

In my last year of college I got a job working for the General Motors Corporation, nearly by accident too. I learned about it from a friend who planned to leave the company to attend seminary.

"Why don't you give me your job?" I asked. I meant it as a joke.

"Do you really want it?" he asked.

"Well, yes!" I replied.

"Then come downtown tomorrow and apply. I'll tell them to expect you."

I could hardly believe my good fortune.

My job with General Motors, trudging up and down the floors of the company's world headquarters in downtown Detroit delivering telegrams, wasn't any more challenging than the work of vacuuming, but I liked the hours better and the company paid my college tuition. Plus, I got to wear a tie to work! I felt like I'd won the lottery.

The General Motors Building was a study in itself. One of the grand old buildings in the city of Detroit, it was built in the 1920s and had more than a million square feet and five thousand windows. Each floor is laid out in eight wings, with a long central corridor connecting them. Although all the floors looked similar, each had its own culture. There were the computer technicians in their white lab coats in the basement, who always seemed glad to see me. A few floors up the sales managers greeted one another in the hallway and talked about their golf game. I could feel the competitive tension between them when I stepped out of the elevator.

High above us all, like the gods of Olympus, the president and vice presidents were housed on the fourteenth floor. Visitors gained access to their wing by passing through a large glass door that served as a kind of veil into the holy of holies of the corporation. All who entered there underwent the scrutiny of a stern security guard. This floor was a place of dark wood, restaurant-dim light, and an atmosphere heavy with important decisions. Intimidated, I passed through those offices like a ghost, rarely speaking and barely noticed.

I could see that the executives on the fourteenth floor were a breed apart. They rode to work in company cars chauffeured by personal drivers and ate lunch in a private dining room. There was even an executive bathroom. On his first day on the job, a fellow messenger made the mistake of using their facility while delivering telegrams. Within seconds a row of neatly polished shoes appeared at the bottom of the stall, followed by a discreet tap at the door.

"Sir, we would like a word with you when you are finished," an authoritative voice said.

When he opened the stall door, two stern security guards stood outside. They gripped him by both arms, the guards positioned on either side like bookends, and silently escorted him to the main hallway where the elevators are located.

"In the future, we'd appreciate it if you used the restrooms on one of the other floors," they said, watching until the elevator doors closed and he descended once again to the regions below where ordinary mortals dwelt.

The work ethic at GM was different from the one I learned at Jack-in-the-Box. When I finished my delivery run early and returned to the office, someone took me aside and quietly told me I needed to walk slower on my route and find something to fill the forty-five minutes allotted for each run before coming back to the office. There was a coffeeshop on the main floor that sold donuts and a bookstore in the building across the street. Failing that, he showed me a back room where supplies were kept. If all else failed, I could hide there until a respectable amount of time passed.

When I transferred to another division in the company to work in the mail room, I discovered the same mentality. Eager to prove myself to my supervisor, I sorted through the mountain of envelopes and magazines as quickly as I could, sliding each one into its assigned slot. My boss noticed my zeal and called me into his office.

"You need to slow down," he said. "You're getting done too soon and making the others look bad."

At first I bristled at his suggestion and then was amazed at how easy I found it to comply. Soon I spent most of the day teaching myself to read Latin and scanning the magazines before they were delivered. The greatest demand was the challenge of filling the tedium between mail runs with activities that looked like they might be related to my work. I dreamed of quitting and doing something more meaningful with my life.

Eventually, I got my wish and entered the realm of "vocational ministry." To my surprise I found ministry was not so different from work. The competitiveness of the sales managers, the tedium of the mail room, and even the privilege of the fourteenth floor were all present. Like the sales managers I saw at General Motors, many of the pastors I met were eager to be the most successful in their "territory." Whenever I met another pastor for the first time at a conference or some professional meeting, the opening question was always the same: "How big is your church?" It embarrassed me to admit my church was small. The boredom I felt while sorting letters as a mail clerk was matched by the slow rhythm of life in a rural church.

But there were also privileges that came with being the pastor of a church. For the most part, people treated me with respect as the church's "minister." I was master of my own schedule, able to come and go as I pleased. I was close enough to home to be there for many of the major events in my children's development, like their first word or their first step. Most of all, I enjoyed the incredible privilege of being paid to study the Bible for hours at a time.

Some days I felt driven by the ambition to succeed almost to the point where the thought of it consumed me night and day. At other times I drifted along listlessly, working hard at looking busy. Most of the time it was just work. I should not have been surprised. Ministry is work, and work when viewed rightly is ministry. Ministry is just another word for service, and all legitimate labor can be offered to God as a form of service. "Work," Eugene Peterson has observed, "is the primary context for our spirituality."

Now I work for a Christian organization whose mission is to train students for vocational ministry. We are not training our students to become airline pilots or engineers but for something we call full-time Christian service. I believe in our mission but fear at times it may give students the wrong impression. I want my students to consider ministry a high calling, but I do not want them to believe that it is on a different order than "secular" work. I fear the rhetoric we use may lead them to think the work of ministry differs, both in its dignity and its nature, from "regular" work.

My colleagues are sometimes offended when I refer to what I do as a job. "You shouldn't think of it as a job," they say. "You should view it as a ministry." I do. But I also know it is work. I do not believe this is a bad thing. Men and women have been created to work. They were created in God's image, and God is a worker. The wonders of creation are called the works of his hand (Ps. 8:6). He finished them in six days and "rested from all his work" on the seventh. According to Jesus, he continues to work "to this very day" (John 5:17).

Jesus, too, was no stranger to the world of work. Prior to beginning his public ministry he submitted himself to the daily grind. He did not think it beneath him to work for a living and was called "the Carpenter" long before anyone ever addressed him as Rabbi or Messiah (Mark 6:3).

Like Christ, the apostle Paul also worked with his hands, supporting himself as a tentmaker during his apostolic ministry (Acts 18:3; 1 Cor. 4:12). What is more, Paul commanded the church to follow his example, telling believers to work so they would not have to steal and would have something to share with those who are in need (Acts 20:34–35; Eph. 4:28). Both motives share the same assumption. Those who labor do not work merely for the joy of the task. The workman, whether engaged in secular or sacred employment, expects to be paid (cf. 2 Tim. 2:6). Ministry is work in the best sense of the word. Likewise, work is ministry. By it we render service to man as agents of God. In the Christian vocabulary, work is not a four-letter word.

Both the ordinary ministry of work and the extraordinary work of ministry are subject to the same temptations. I have been no less susceptible to the cold dread of Monday morning or the languid torpor of Friday afternoon as a pastor or a professor than I was when I shuffled through the halls of the GM building. In either calling there have been days when I forced myself to get up and go and times when I felt my occupation was an undeserved gift from God. Experience has shown me that people in ministry do not always do their best and that even Christian employers can sometimes be unfair and unappreciative. What is more, I cannot help noting the irony that God's primary call on my life came not while I was praying at the altar but while I was cooking at the grill, and that my first lessons in spirituality were learned while carrying hot grease from the fryers to the dumpster.

Not long ago my oldest son came home from work, elated about his new job as a sales clerk in a large retail chain. With a wide grin, he declared, "I definitely like this job! I don't have to *do* anything!"

I spoke to him about the virtue of hard work and tried to show him that he was really working for Jesus. Doing his best, I explained, was a way to serve God. He rolled his eyes and listened patiently. I congratulated myself when I was finished, satisfied that I had discharged my spiritual duty as a parent.

Later, I tried to recall all the jobs I'd held over the years and wondered what the next day would be like for me at work. Dreading the sound of the alarm in the morning, I counted the number of days left until the weekend.

CHAPTER 16

A Shepherd of the Flock

On a steamy August day in 1985, I left our apartment in the suburbs of Philadelphia in a U-Haul loaded with all our worldly goods and our little Ford hitched to the back. After four years of seminary, I was eager to begin my ministry as a pastor. At first I felt so nervous about the trip I could barely hold on to the steering wheel. The last words of the attendant at the truck rental agency as he handed us the keys were, "Whatever you do, don't back up!" But after a few hours Jane and I bounced along in the cab quite at ease, marveling at the long shadow we cast.

The green hills of Pennsylvania gave way to the flat land of Ohio, Indiana, and Illinois, and we rolled through miles of corn-fields, past one sleepy little town after another. Each new one looked identical to the ones we left behind a few miles back, with a post office and stop sign in the center of town and the white spire of its church rising high above the houses. The country roads stretched long and straight in front of us until at last we turned up the gravel drive to the place where Jane and I were to spend the next nine years of our lives.

Valley Chapel's parsonage, a red ranch home perched on a low hill, was surrounded by farm land. To someone who grew up with neighbors living close enough to hear our family's arguments, the place was dry and desolate. The wide horizon reminded me of my mother's stories about growing up on the plains of Regina, Canada.

I climbed down from the cab and noticed a tall figure ambling through the field toward us. As I waited for him to reach the truck, I swatted at a tiny bee barely the size of a small fly buzzing around my arm, attracted to the beads of sweat that formed there. The man appeared out of nowhere. I supposed he had been out walking in the field of Christmas trees that surrounded the parsonage, and hoped he was from the church. I was eager to get a key and start unloading the truck. The man, who said his name was John, drew near and stretched out a long arm. With a wide grin he declared, "Welcome home."

I thanked him, still feeling like a visitor, and hoped his words were prophetic. Weeks earlier my wife and I were sitting stiffly on someone's white love seat, answering questions about our background. I was sweating then too, but not from the temperature. I was anxious for these strangers to like me and to see me as their pastor. The names and faces, just a blur then, are all familiar to me now, their voices burned in my memory.

Standing in the drive next to the moving van, John and I exchanged comments about the weather and the bees until a small crowd of people materialized, consisting of most of the congregation. The men swarmed the truck. The women drifted toward the kitchen and started putting away dishes and silverware, chattering happily about the improvements to the parsonage. I wandered through the truck and tried to help the men with the heavy furniture, dazed as much by the unfamiliarity of the place as by the heat. John took me aside and in a confidential tone mentioned the name of someone in the hospital who needed a visit from me. The truck wasn't unloaded yet. I didn't even know where the hospital was.

In what seemed like minutes the job was finished and the people vanished as quickly as they appeared. Jane and I spent the first hour in our new home winding our way through the parsonage exploring its rooms. The house was originally located in town about a mile down the road. The previous owner moved it to this location and added rooms in a meandering floor plan that exhibited little rhyme or reason. Having spent the first six years of our marriage in apartments, the place felt like a mansion to us. We had never lived in a house so large.

I eventually made my way down to my office in the basement of the parsonage and surveyed the confusion. Boxes were stacked to the ceiling. I squeezed between the towering piles to sit at my desk and felt the realization settle over me like Elijah's mantle. Jane and I prayed for this for years. This was why we endured the tedium and loneliness of seminary. I was finally a shepherd of the flock. "What now?" I wondered. They hadn't told me what to do next in seminary. I decided to hang my diploma on the wall, more for my benefit than for anyone else's.

That night as we were about to go to bed, Jane gasped in alarm when something darted across the bedroom carpet in a blur of movement. I suppose we should have expected it. Dave and Sarah, the couple we stayed with when we first visited the church, joked with us about the mousetraps scattered throughout their home. Dave climbed into bed one night and a mouse ran across his chest. Mice were common in these parts. The parsonage, we soon learned, was infested with the tiny creatures. At night we could hear them scratching in the walls and skittering across the ceiling in the kitchen. We eventually named one of the storage areas in the basement the "mouse room." A kind of elephant's graveyard for rodents, it was one of their primary entry points and often the place where they went to die after we poisoned them. We entered the mouse room only when absolutely necessary and always with a sense of foreboding.

Betty, one of the women in the church, felt sympathetic toward mice and left food for them in her garage during the winter. Jane and I, on the other hand, felt no such compassion. We were firm in our conviction it was better to smell a dead mouse than to see a live one.

The thought that she might have to share her bedroom with mice was more than Jane could bear on that first night in our new home. Keeping her eyes peeled, she took one of the newly emptied suitcases. "I'm not staying here," she declared and started to fill it with clothing. Armed with a tennis racquet lest any of our unwelcome visitors should suddenly appear, I reasoned with her.

"Where are you going to stay?" I said. "We can't go back to Detroit. I've already told them I'll be their pastor."

"I don't know," she said. "But I won't stay in the same house with mice!"

Her threat was mere bravado, of course. Jane knew as well as I did that she didn't have any other choice. Our lot was cast with the church and we were in it for the long haul, mice or no mice. Resigning herself to the inevitable, she climbed up onto the bed and nervously scanned the floor. We turned out the light and listened to the clamor in the walls, waiting for sleep to come and tense from the strangeness of trying to sleep in a new place.

Mice, we soon discovered, were not the only form of wildlife we had to cope with in our new surroundings. A jaybird that had its nest among the trees surrounding the parsonage concluded we were trespassers in its domain. It stalked me whenever I walked down the long drive to the road to pick up the mail. Chattering angrily, it hovered above my head as if it were a hawk about to drop on its prey. I kept my eyes on the ground as it circled, watching for its shadow. I wondered alternately if I was only imagining it or if it might swoop down and pluck out my eyes.

During one of my treks the bird finally decided it was no longer enough to chatter imprecations. When I reached the road, it dove. I made a dash for the house, flailing my arms and screaming, certain I could feel the beat of its wings on my neck all the way up the house drive. Once inside I looked out the window and saw it station itself on a wire high above the mailbox, as if waiting for my return. The mail was still in the box.

There were snakes in the grass too. I nearly fainted one day when I almost stepped on a huge bull snake in the back yard. Up to that point the only snakes I saw outside the zoo were tiny. This one was several feet long and looked like a boa constrictor to me. I might have felt better had I known bull snakes are harmless and usually eat mice. But I could only think of scenes from the Tarzan movies I watched as a child, in which the giant snake wraps itself around its hapless victim, usually some bespectacled member of the safari who had no business being in the jungle, and slowly chokes the life out of him.

Although technically not wildlife, the hogs next door made us nervous too. In the evenings, Jane and I liked to walk down the country road that bordered the church's property. One day a herd of hogs owned by one of our neighbors suddenly appeared in the field across the road after the corn was harvested. He put them out to graze among the stubble for the winter. We'd never lived next door to hogs before and decided to get a closer look. We were amazed by their size. These were not the cute curly tailed creatures we saw in cartoons but great hulking slabs that looked like they could crush us. I thought nervously about the gospel story in which a legion of demons drove a herd of swine over a cliff.

A flimsy wire was all that separated us from the herd. We discovered later that this was an electrified fence, a formidable barrier the hogs learned to respect through unfortunate experience. But to us it hardly looked capable of stopping such great beasts. When the hogs saw us coming down the road, they moved *en masse* in our direction, grunting in a way that sounded vaguely threatening. They were just excited, of course, having concluded we were there to feed them. We were unschooled in the ways of swine and had no way of knowing this. Trying not to run, out of fear it might compel them to give chase, we quickly turned around and hurried back to the house.

Jane and I took steps to deal with these threats. We scattered hedge apples, the rumpled fruit of the Osage orange tree, in the mouse room and hung an inflatable snake in the garage. No one could explain what it was about hedge apples, a plant in the mulberry family, that mice didn't like. We put a screen over the downspout to keep the bull snake from hiding there. I went to the mailbox wearing a baseball cap and carrying an umbrella for protection. We learned to live with the hogs.

The people, however, were another matter. The residents of this small community were as much a puzzle to us as we were to them. They waved when they drove by in the car but sat in silence when we walked into the diner. When we showed up at sporting events, they stared from a distance as if we were an unknown species but treated us with studied disinterest when we came closer. I asked one of the older members of our church how long it took for people in town to accept newcomers. "I've lived here for twenty years, and they still look at me as an outsider," she said. "I think you have to be born here."

My role as a pastor didn't help matters. It made people nervous to learn what I did. I visited a woman in the community who told me she worried all day knowing I was coming. She was so anxious she cleaned the closets in her home. When I asked her why, she said, "Having the minister come over is almost like having God visit your house." Another family I visited told me their little daughter burst into tears when they told her the preacher was coming over. "But Mommy," she cried, "I don't want the creature to come over." As far as I was concerned, that about said it all. I wasn't a person anymore. I was "the creature."

While my identity as a pastor made people outside the church ill at ease, those who were a part of the church felt differently. Church members always mentioned my title when they introduced me to their friends and neighbors. "This is our minister, Reverend Koessler," they said. The title always came before the name. In personal conversation some omitted my name altogether, addressing me only as "Preacher." The sound of it always brought me up short, like a slap or a sharp blast of cold air, the stark language a blunt reminder of their expectations. Still, whatever pride the congregation felt in having me as their pastor was mixed with a healthy dose of skepticism. I may have been their minister, but I was also a rookie who needed to prove himself.

The Sunday after we arrived, I found one of the church elders after the service and told him I wanted to schedule a board meeting as soon as possible. "I want to start making plans for the future," I explained. Eager to cast a vision for the church, I already had some long-range goals in mind.

"Yes, that would be good," the elder replied. "Plus, we have to negotiate your salary." I blinked for a moment, not comprehending.

"What do you mean?" I asked.

"We need to decide how much we are going to pay you."

The question of salary came up during my candidacy and the board gave me a printout of the previous pastor's salary package. It was modest but enough for us to make ends meet. Now it looked as if I had misunderstood. Did they really think I'd moved halfway across the country without knowing my salary?

Apparently, they did. It was also apparent the board planned to pay me less than the previous pastor. When I told them of my assumption that my salary was the same as the former pastor's, the treasurer was incredulous. "The last pastor was here for eight years," he said. "Why should we pay you the same, when you are just starting out?" After a long and uncomfortable discussion, the board reluctantly agreed to match the previous pastor's salary. This was not an auspicious beginning.

The church's leaders expressed similar skepticism when I presented my long-term goals to them. I laid them out with neat precision in a chart that linked each goal to one of the church's four functions: worship, fellowship, evangelism, and discipleship. I expected them to be impressed. Instead, the board members looked quizzically at one another after I distributed the document. There was a long pause. They looked at each other again and then at me. Finally someone spoke up. "For the life of me, I can't understand why you put evangelism on this list."

One member offered a suggestion for improving my messages. "If you can't say it in twenty minutes," he told me as he shook my hand after the sermon, "it doesn't need to be said." He smiled to let me know he was merely trying to be helpful. Some of the criticisms I received were warranted, like the time one of the church's elders took me to task for the tone of my voice. "Sometimes, when you preach, you sound like you're angry with us," he said. I was defensive in my response but later admitted that he was right. Like an overachieving father whose children's best accomplishments can never measure up to his expectation, there were times when I was disappointed with the congregation. I knew it was a good little church. It just wasn't what I imagined for myself when I dreamed of the glory of ministry back in seminary. I changed my tone.

Despite this, the church was genuinely grateful to have me as their pastor. People thanked me for my messages and sometimes told me how God spoke to them through the sermon. One couple invited us out to their home on Friday nights for dinner. Afterward we talked about the church and prayed for God's blessing. Occasionally someone stopped by and asked for counsel. I spent my days working on sermons and stepped into the pulpit on Sunday to preach them.

The study and the pulpit were the two places I felt most at home. My heart beat faster when I sat at my desk with my books spread out in front of me. The high point of the week was the moment I walked up the steps to the pulpit muttering to the Holy Spirit for his blessing and began to preach. Afterward the congregation smiled and shook my hand on the way out, even when they disagreed.

For a time I attempted to make inroads into the community by dropping in at the diner but was unnerved by the silent stares I received. A group of farmers in overalls and seed caps sat in the middle of the restaurant harassing the waitress, a weather-beaten woman who called them all "honey." They gave me sidelong glances when I sat at their table. Someone muttered, "We'd better watch what we say now." It was clear my presence changed the atmosphere. A moment earlier they were laughing and talking among themselves. Now there was only awkward silence. I asked a few questions to try to restart the conversation, but they weren't having any of it. My comments were met with grunts or one-word replies. I sat there for about twenty minutes, nursing a bitter cup of coffee and trying to look friendly, then finally got up. They might have warmed up to me had I persevered. But I felt too intimidated. My stomach churned when I thought of making the visit again. I tried a few more times and then gave up.

It wasn't much better when I visited church members in their homes. They were always friendly when I showed up and welcomed me with cookies and sweet tea. I know I appeared reticent to them.

I was merely tongue-tied and self-conscious. It wasn't their fault; I place the blame on myself. I was hampered by my fundamental incapacity for small talk, the relational thread that runs through the social fabric of a group and knits it together. I could talk about the Bible or matters of the soul well enough, but when the conversation turned to things like the rivalry between the Cubs and the Cardinals or the condition of the crops, I floundered, uncertain as a ship cast on the waves of a stormy sea.

Hospital visits were even worse, but for a different reason. In the hospital, medical personnel moved through the halls with an air of grim purpose as bedfast patients gazed with hollow eyes through darkened doorways. Whenever I stepped through the hospital doors I felt unnerved by the cold aroma of lives hanging in the balance, and I was intimidated by the gravity of the circumstances. In that place small talk became a necessary anchor, a lifeline to keep me from drifting away on the waves of my own fear. The subject of the mundane was a refuge, not a burden, in the hospital. It provided a moment or two of relief when everyone could pretend things were normal. When the small talk ended, I gingerly pulled the veil of idle chatter aside and turned to face the disease.

I quailed every time I did this, overwhelmed by my own impotency. Past experience proved I did not possess the gift of healing. Unlike the doctors and nurses who came equipped with pills and procedures, all I could offer the sick and dying were words. If there was power in them, it was beyond me. I opened the Bible and read a passage usually chosen for its suitability to the sufferer's condition. Then I grasped the patient by the hand and prayed. There was no perceptible change in the condition of the afflicted when I did this. The lame did not take up their mats and walk. The blind did not see. Yet each time a light was kindled in the eyes of those who heard, even in those who knew they were dying. Somehow my voice, which sounded hollow and reedy to my ears as it reverberated against the walls of the hospital room, became the voice of God to them. Those were the moments that caused me to question my calling the most, as well as the ones that confirmed it. In those moments, I felt least effective and most like a pastor.

Still, I wondered whether it was a mistake to settle in a rural community. I came to Valley Chapel with high hopes, confident that in a short time I could transform this small congregation of less than fifty people into a church of several hundred. But after two years we weren't much bigger than when I arrived. There were rumblings when the board called for a congregational vote to change a key element in the church's constitution. Although the proposal was supported by a majority of the congregation, those who opposed the motion felt I manipulated the church's leaders.

All of this coincided with the death of my father. I came back from the funeral to a congregational meeting in which hard words were spoken. Someone suggested the vote was rigged. I was angry about my father and hurt by the accusation. I started sending out my resume, hoping to find a church that was a better fit. The congregation that responded was near my hometown. A church with multiple staff that was three times as large as Valley Chapel, it was close to my family, and there were no hogs in sight. The church was made to order for us.

However, as the date approached for us to candidate at the church, I began to have doubts about the move. Subtle clues suggested the change might not be much of a change after all. In one of my phone conversations with the chairman of the search committee, the subject of salary came up. "We're wondering what you are being paid at your current church," he asked. When I gave him the figures, he explained why it was important. "We don't want to offer you too little," he said. Then after a pause he added, "But we also don't want to offer you too much."

I contacted one of the church's former pastors and asked him about his experience. He was emphatic in his answer: "John, I wouldn't wish that church on my worst enemy." That couldn't be a good sign. Neither was the search-committee chairman's assurance that I could fire any of the pastoral staff I wanted once I became the senior pastor. He meant to reassure me that I had the board's support if I accepted the call, but it only made me nervous about their loyalty to the pastoral staff.

The clincher came when I visited the church to candidate. I'm not sure whether it was a trick of the light or simply my imagination, but during the question-and-answer period after the sermon, I peered out at the audience and saw the faces of my congregation in Green Valley. It wasn't guilt I felt so much as a sense of longing. In the dim light of another church's sanctuary my congregation felt more comfortable and familiar to me. Suddenly taking a new church didn't seem like such a good idea.

When I was ordained, the pastor who organized the service asked that a single chair be placed on the platform. It was there not for me to sit on but to lean on. "You wouldn't believe how heavy the weight is when they lay hands on you and pray," he explained. The real weight, I discovered, came later, after the service ended and I assumed the mantle of pastoral responsibility. That weight compelled me to return to Valley Chapel and drove me back to my knees again and again as I tried to shepherd the flock God called me to serve.

Years after the experience I learned that the search committee believed I turned down their offer because I felt I was too good for their church. They were wrong. I turned it down because I realized Valley Chapel was God's best for me.

CHAPTER 17

Out of the Ordinary

I wasn't expecting much from the old man. With a grandfather's white hair and a funeral director's black suit, he stepped into the pulpit with the tentativeness of age. The crowd of more than a thousand beamed as he acknowledged their long applause with a smile.

I'd heard his name before. He was the pastor of one of the largest churches in the nation, a successful author, and a renowned speaker. But I was skeptical, aggravated by his popularity.

"Probably overrated," I thought to myself, shifting uncomfortably in my narrow seat.

The auditorium was old like him, steaming from humidity and the sweat of the audience. I was homesick, missing my wife and feeling insignificant among the vast crowd of pastors who attended the conference. The parade of celebrities across the platform made me feel like a failure.

I listened absently as the old pastor spoke. He was approaching the end of his long ministry, and during his message he reflected on his experiences. As he moved toward the conclusion he began to list some of the benefits he enjoyed as a pastor. He described the free suits one of the members of his church purchased for him and the free car provided for his use. He mentioned the beautiful house in which he lived at the church's expense and the generous salary his church offered.

The list was long and impressive enough to make me, the pastor of a small and struggling church, both envious and cynical. I grew increasingly uncomfortable as he continued because I could tell where all this was heading. "What if I had not been given all these benefits?" he was going to ask. "Would I still serve my Lord?"

I knew the answer. He was going to say, "I have searched my heart, and by God's grace, I believe I would."

My clothes were limp with humidity and I hunkered down in my hard seat in the upper balcony, wishing I hadn't come. I wasn't very happy about how things were going at the church, and I had come to the conference harboring a secret hope I might be able to make some connections that opened the door to a different place of ministry. The last thing I wanted to hear about was his large salary, free suits, free car, and beautiful manse.

Sure enough, the question I dreaded finally came. "What if I had never been given all these things?" the speaker boomed. "Would I still serve my Lord?" The air hung heavy with anticipation as the crowd waited for his reply, and I slumped a little lower in my seat. There was a long, long pause.

"I don't know. God help me," he said. Then he left the platform.

I was shocked.

I was devastated.

I was convicted.

I avoided the ice-cream social afterward and went to my room. Once there, I fell on my knees and begged God for help, because I knew he spoke the truth about me too. I began to wonder how I was ever going to make it to the end of my own course. It was early in my ministry and I felt like I was already faltering. What possible hope could there be for later on? How could I find my way?

Twenty years later I stood on the platform in the same auditorium. The seats were filled with college students, men and women preparing for a lifetime of ministry who shifted restlessly in the narrow seats and absently wondered what I had to say. Their questions echoed in counterpoint, reverberating with those I asked that night in my room. Am I really doing what God wants me to do? How will I find my way? The answer is clear to me now, discovered first while I was on my knees reflecting on the old man's sermon.

It is a matter of duty.

"What pastors do, or at least are called to do," Eugene Peterson writes, "is really quite simple. We say the word of God accurately, so that congregations of Christians can stay in touch with the basic realities of their existence, so they know what is going on. And we say the Name personally, alongside our parishioners in the actual circumstances of their lives, so they will recognize and respond to the God who is both on our side and at our side when it doesn't seem like it and when we don't feel like it."

This was my duty as a pastor. To stand before God's people, as one who proclaims God's Word, and beside God's people, as one who lives it out with them. It is not so different from what I am called to do now that I am no longer a pastor. To some extent, it is no different from what God expects of all believers. To stand with one another as members of the same household of faith. To listen to what God has said. To speak the truth in love to one another.

But having a sense of duty does not simply mean focusing on the right things. It also includes a sense of being "in place." There is a military dimension to it. We are "on duty" until we have been given liberty to leave.

During the first few years of my pastoral ministry, I had several opportunities to change churches. Most of them were "better" opportunities — larger congregations, more staff, closer to family. Often they were opportunities I solicited. In most cases the thing that kept me from accepting a call, even when I wanted to say yes, was the lack of a sense of release. This is admittedly subjective. But I did not feel I could go until I sensed that the Holy Spirit said, "You are dismissed."

I do not think this is unique to those who are in ministry. We are all placed in a variety of contexts that require us to "do our duty." Our roles as husbands and wives, sons and daughters, employers and employees all have a vocational dimension.

What God calls us to do may be simple, but that does not mean it is easy. Our path is fraught with difficulties and our most common companion is often a feeling of inadequacy. That is why a sense of duty must be accompanied by a healthy sense of self.

When I was a pastor I learned congregational expectations are often unreasonably high. People want a pastor who is as purpose driven as Rick Warren, as entrepreneurial as Bill Hybels, as evangelistic as Billy Graham, and as compassionate as Mother Teresa.

They want a wise leader, someone who has easy answers to the complex problems of the church.

They want a charismatic leader. The ideal pastor is someone who can get the church to do what it doesn't want to do and make them believe they like it.

They want a dynamic leader. One into whose hands they can place the shards of their shattered lives and then receive them back again whole.

What did they get instead?

Someone like me.

Not the wisest.

Not the bravest.

Not the holiest.

The best they could expect was an ordinary person. I should not have been surprised. To paraphrase Abraham Lincoln, God must love to use ordinary people, he calls so many of them!

Watson Thornton was one of those people. I met Watson when he was in his eighties. He walked in off the street looking for a place to worship closer to his home, and our little church somehow attracted his attention. Watson grew up on the mission field in Japan, the son of a pastor who was himself the son of a pastor. When the time came to decide on a career, he made the obvious choice. He decided to become a farmer!

One day, however, during a chapel service at the college where Watson attended, the Lord began to deal with him. He sensed God wanted him to be a pastor. "Lord," Watson prayed, "I don't want to be a pastor. I want to be a farmer." But the Lord seemed to say, "Watson, I want you to be a pastor."

When the chapel service ended and the rest of the students filed out, Watson remained in his seat, deep in prayer. "Lord," he complained, "I don't want to be a pastor. I want to be a farmer."

Still, he felt the gentle urging of the Spirit, as the Lord insisted, "Watson, I want you to be a pastor."

Finally, late in the evening, still sitting in the darkened chapel, Watson gave in. "Okay, Lord," he prayed. "Have it your way. But I want you to know you are losing a very good farmer and gaining a very poor pastor!"

He went on to have a ministry of building up several failing churches in southern Illinois and later served as a missionary to Japan. During several of those years, he worked to support himself. As a farmer.

Watson was a mentor to me during my years at Valley Chapel. I tried to visit him weekly and listened to his stories. His devotion to the Word impressed me. Even at that late stage in his life Watson was still an avid student of Scripture. He determined to finish his life studying the book of Revelation, and every time I visited him he spoke of some new insight. He told me remarkable stories of God's leading in his ministry, the kind you read about in missionary biographies. Yet he never lost the sense he was just a farmer God decided to use.

Watson helped me to see that having a healthy sense of myself was a matter of being realistic about ministry. It was a matter of knowing where I was strong, where I was weak, and where I could get by. It meant building my ministry on my strengths, striving for competency in the areas where I just got by, and pleading for mercy in my areas of weakness.

I do not feel much more competent as a college professor than I did as a pastor. Nor, for that matter, do I feel extraordinary as a husband and father. But I know what is expected of me and have some sense of what I do best and where I need help. These are not ministry-specific requirements. The executive in her office and the truck driver in his rig are as dependent upon God as the pastor in his study or the monk in his cell. If any of us experiences a measure of success in what we do, it should come as something of a surprise. It is a gift of grace.

John Newton once wrote, "If you had the talents of an angel, you could do no good with them till His hour is come, and till He leads you to the people whom He has determined to bless by your means." If Newton is correct, much of what I think I could be doing, if I were just given the chance, could be wrong. In the end, the secret to all success is grace.

More than a decade ago, through an unusual combination of prayer and divinely arranged coincidence, the Lord made it clear it was time for me to leave the church I served for nine years and join the Pastoral Studies Department of the Moody Bible Institute. During my last month at the church, I attended a local ministerial meeting and was approached by a fellow pastor who heard about the opportunity. First, he offered his congratulations. Then, flushing a little with embarrassment, he said, "Don't take this the wrong way. But I just have to ask ... Why you?"

I know what he meant. Had I been in his shoes, I'd have asked the same question (though perhaps not aloud). In fact, I often ask it of the Lord when I notice someone who seems to me to be doing something more glamorous or attractive than what I am doing. I take a sidelong glance at their success, the way some men gaze in secret envy at another man's wife, and think to myself, "Lord, why him and not me?"

I am ashamed to admit this. Such an attitude makes anyone who has better gifts, a more appealing opportunity, or greater outward success a rival, rather than a brother or sister in Christ.

So why them and not me? Or why me and not them? The answer is simple. It is a matter of grace. It is a result of God's purpose and the ministry of the Holy Spirit, who alone has the sovereign right to dispense gifts and opportunities as he sees fit.

I am learning I need to be careful about rushing to judgment about my potential in life and ministry. I don't really know where or how God plans to use me in the future. Neither should I be too quick to draw conclusions about the value of the ministry which I have already accomplished. I see only faces, not hearts. I may hear words of praise or criticism, but I cannot discern the still small voice of conviction that burns within the hearts of those who hear what I preach or read what I write. I hope I know what God is doing through me. I often think I know what God wants to do. But I will not truly know until the day of Christ reveals it.

I must be equally cautious about drawing false conclusions about the blessings God grants. It is tempting to interpret the good things that come into my life as marks of divine favor and hardship as signs of God's displeasure. Jesus' tortured cry upon the cross is proof that suffering says little about God's favor.

This is why we must walk the pilgrim's path with a sense of expectation. I must be realistic in my expectations and confident of the reward to come afterward. Both are critical because the call to discipleship is a call to suffering as well as reward.

It is a call to suffering because what was true of the master will be true of the servant. Jesus suffered and so will his disciples. Of course, it's not the suffering that surprises me so much as the context. Often the place of our greatest discomfort is the church. We come to it for refuge and leave feeling like outsiders. We suffer more at the hands of our friends than we ever have from those who are our enemies.

Speaker and author Kathleen Norris wrestled with this question when she was trying to decide whether to join a church. She was helped in her decision by the blunt assessment of a Benedictine monk. "The church," he said, "is still a sinful institution. How could it be otherwise?"

Norris writes that his words startled her into a "recognition of simple truth." "The church," she explains, "is a human institution, full of ordinary people, sinners like me, who say and do stupid things." The key phrase is "sinners like me."

So why do we still bother with a church that has caused us so much grief? It is because we have no other choice. Where else would we go? What else would we do? How can we give up now, when there is so much to be gained?

If life and ministry aren't very glorious, it is because the glory comes later. My problem is that I want it now. And because I want it now, I am sometimes tempted to sell it short and settle for a lesser glory. I am tempted to seek a new and "better" church or vocation. Or worse, I settle for sex, money, cheap praise, or perhaps just another half hour of sleep. We think the trouble is that we are disappointed with ministry when the real problem, as C. S. Lewis once observed, is that we are "far too easily pleased."

The apostle Paul, writing of his own ministry struggles, observed, "Our light and momentary troubles are achieving for us an eternal glory that far outweighs them all" (2 Cor. 4:17). The old King James version puts it more graphically, when it speaks of "a far more exceeding and eternal weight of glory."

Just what is this glory that is so luminous that it will cause all our troubles to pale in comparison? It is the gift of hearing Christ call us by name on the last day. It is the gift not only of seeing Christ in glory but of seeing that we are a reflection of that glory. Most of all, it is the gift of looking back over the long and toilsome years of our lives and seeing all we have done refracted through God's grace like light through a prism. Only then will we discover all the beauty, blessing, and reward now hidden from our sight.

CHAPTER 18

Sacred Spaces

The church I served as pastor originally met in a storefront located on the same corner that hosted our town's only stop sign. The building had once been a mom-and-pop grocery store. The "mom" was Minnie, who still lived next door in the building that once housed Green Valley's most popular diner. She slept in the back but kept the grill, tables, chairs, and soda fountain out front. Minnie stopped serving years ago. The diner was now sacred space, a shrine to the way things used to be.

Minnie's walls were covered with grainy photos of girls in poodle skirts with bobbed hair and of young boys with brush cuts. When visiting, the older members of my congregation pointed to the faces and recited the names as if repeating a liturgy we both knew. As a stranger to the place, the images meant nothing to me. Then, with a shy smile, the visitors inevitably pointed to a figure in one of the photographs. A younger version of their own likeness, frozen in time.

The photos recalled a better time, the days when the town had its own car dealer and tavern. The tavern burned down under mysterious circumstances, and the town seemed destined to follow, dying not by fire but by slow strangulation. Like most of the nation's rural communities in the 1980s, Green Valley reeled in the aftermath of the farming-industry collapse. Everyone knew at least one person who had filed for bankruptcy, gone insane, or committed suicide.

I was blissfully ignorant of all of this. But there were clues for those who knew how to interpret the signs. I mean that literally. There were "for sale" signs in front of many of the homes in town. Most had been on the market for months. Some for a year or more.

I suppose I should have suspected something when members of the pulpit committee took us for a drive to see the "area." Instead of showing us around town, we drove forty-five minutes north to the "rich" section of Peoria. I liked the neighborhood's suburban feel. It didn't dawn on me that it was nowhere near where I would be living. It probably wouldn't have mattered anyway. I was just out of seminary and anxious to find a church — any church — that would have me as its pastor.

Stepping through the door to Minnie's was like going back in time. It offered a brief respite from the blunt reality of the present. And if Minnie's place was a sanctuary, then she herself was its priestess, speaking like prophetess Huldah with oracular authority.

The building where our church met was also sacred space, set apart by the presence of our congregation each Sunday. It was just a room, really, not much bigger than a large living room. The white walls, plastic folding chairs, and old air conditioner jutting out of the wall gave the place a stark, no-nonsense atmosphere that appealed to the church's members.

The sign on the window was hand painted in old English letters by one of our members. It bore the name of our church, the pastor's name, and the time of our Sunday service. When I became the new pastor, they left the letters of the previous pastor's name that matched my own and painted over the others. The result, with some letters written large and others squeezed into a space which they did not quite fit, appeared slightly distorted.

The building's most notable feature was its lack of bathrooms. This deficiency did not pose a problem for church members, who were prepared to wait until after the service. Visitors, however, were a different matter. Should one ask how to find the restroom, he or she was told to go next door, knock at Minnie's place, and ask to use her bathroom. She always gave them a gracious welcome, but the embarrassment often proved too much for strangers. Most of those who passed through this initiation did not return. Those who did come back learned to wait.

This did not bother our members. They viewed our lack of facilities as a test of loyalty to Christ. After all, if a person is too embarrassed to knock at someone's door and ask to go to the bathroom, they might also be too ashamed to take a stand for Jesus. Like the early monks who considered monasticism a form of living martyrdom, worship without bathrooms was a holy sacrifice. A strong bladder was a mark of grace.

This ended when we constructed our own church building. Technically the building was what local farmers refer to as a pole shed. The church's walls were built at the factory. We cheered as the first one rose into place, and I thought of Nehemiah repairing the walls of Jerusalem with a sword strapped to his side. We watched ours go up while drinking lemonade on the parsonage lawn.

These prefabricated walls were no less precious to us than those Nehemiah labored over. And we too faced setbacks, though none as intimidating as the obstacles Nehemiah overcame. Ours mostly concerned the irritations that come with delay and decorating. The gravest involved the theft of our steeple, purchased from a company in the Bible Belt and trucked up north to our church. The driver spent the night in a hotel in Peoria, and when he awoke the next morning his truck was missing. Police located it a few hours later in the Methodist church parking lot—minus the steeple!

None of us held the Methodists personally responsible, though we were suspicious of their doctrine. The police eventually spotted the steeple lying in a ditch near the expressway. The contractor recovered it and set it atop the church. The perpetrators of the crime were never identified.

Some things did not change with the new building. Harry and Theresa, the oldest couple in our congregation, still sat in the last row on the aisle. They claimed the space before the pews were even installed. The front row remained empty, as usual. Most of the congregation claimed spots roughly equivalent to those they inhabited in the old building. With fourteen pews in all, seven on each side, the sanctuary looked cavernous compared with the storefront. In the old building one merely needed to look in a person's direction and speak your mind. On Sunday we were face to face with everyone else in the church. In the new sanctuary, we had to make a concerted effort to see one another. It was now possible to slip in and out of the service unnoticed, something that never happened in the old Valley Chapel.

The change of location was unnerving at first, like waking up one morning and finding yourself in someone else's house. The days in the old building became the "good old days." We looked back on them the way a married couple does the days spent in their first apartment, its austerity softened by the memory of first love. Still, it didn't take long for us to warm up to the new building and to stake out the territory. A few of the ladies took possession of the kitchen. The Sunday school superintendent claimed the library. I got the pastor's office, the smallest room in the building, if you don't count the utility closet. I also laid claim to the two small pews on the sanctuary platform. They became the focus of our first territorial dispute.

The pews were for those who led the worship service. Since it was usually me, I felt I should have primary say in their placement. I knew exactly where I wanted them. I wanted the pews in the center of the platform, with one just to the left and the other just to the right of the pulpit. Looking back on it, I am not sure why I felt so strongly about this. At the time, I told myself it was a matter of decorum and convenience. I took great care to position the two pews exactly where I wanted them. But the next day when I came to the church they were pushed back against the wall. I dragged them to the middle of the platform, took several minutes making sure they were centered, and then went to my office. When I checked on the pews the next day, I saw they had been moved again. I dragged them back to the center of the platform. Then, muttering to myself, I went back to my office to study. The next day the pews were once again moved back against the wall.

Finally, at the conclusion of the board meeting that week, one of the elders said, "We need to talk about the pulpit furniture." I suspected his mother-in-law, who was also the choir director, was the one who moved the pews. He explained that the choir needed more space for its Sunday performances. We discussed the matter quietly for a few minutes until I realized someone was shouting. With dismay, I recognized the voice as my own.

"I am the pastor of this church," I said. "I am the one who is going to spend most of the service on the platform. I want the pews in the center!" Somehow, platform space symbolized the authority of my pastoral position to me. Giving in to the choir director's wishes was as good as giving up my authority. I was called to be the pastor of this church, and, by God, I was determined to be its pastor.

At the time I thought it was important to take control of the situation. Now it just seems silly. God probably did not care where we placed the pews, and the choir director's request was perfectly reasonable. But that is the trouble with sacred space. Sometimes its sacredness comes from the value God invests in it. As with Moses, God manifests his presence in scrub and brush and it becomes holy ground. Before he showed up it was just another patch of desert. Or God shows up in an obscure Jebusite village and calls it his own, and suddenly it becomes the holy city of Jerusalem. But more often than not, sacred space becomes holy ground because of the value we place upon it. It is our presence there that makes it precious to us.

Church buildings are not the only places congregations consider to be sacred space. At a workshop, a pastor once asked me, "What do you do when the church won't tear down the outhouse?" I laughed and said, "I guess you leave it up." "No," he insisted, "I'm serious. What do you do when they won't tear down the outhouse? Our church has an old outhouse on land that we need for parking, but they won't tear it down."

The church had indoor plumbing; nobody used the outhouse anymore. Yet somehow the building was precious to the congregation. Perhaps it reminded them of a "simpler" era. Or maybe, like the old building Minnie rented to us, it was a symbol of sacrifice. Possibly the more pragmatic among them felt the old outhouse was a good backup plan in case the plumbing went bad in the church. Whatever the reason, the outhouse was invested with value that remained a mystery to the pastor. So it was with the platform chairs. For some reason even I did not fully understand, they were precious to me.

When I left the pastorate for a ministry of teaching, I no longer worshiped on the platform. Instead, I sat in pews with the congregation of a different church and grieved. During worship I gazed longingly at the platform and wished I were back in my old pews. I felt lost and out of place.

Some of this, no doubt, was a natural result of changing my ministry role. I felt disoriented moving from the pulpit to the pew. But there was also a physical dimension to my experience. After nearly a decade in front of the congregation, it felt odd to be in their midst once again. I felt hemmed in.

The change came home to me when I returned to Valley Chapel after moving to a different ministry context. The building was unchanged. There were still fourteen pews, seven on each side. Yet what was once spacious to me now felt horribly constricted. Had the church always been this small? How could I not have noticed? It was only when I looked behind me at the windows that separated the sanctuary from the fellowship hall beyond that I realized what made the difference.

When I worshiped on the platform, my field of vision encompassed the entire church. I saw every face, even those I did not want to see. I saw beyond the sanctuary where we worshiped into the fellowship area beyond. I saw the Sunday school rooms and the people who wandered in and out of the sanctuary during the service. I watched the children when they grew bored and played in the aisle. I saw the men who worked or played too hard the night before as they started to nod off during the sermon. It gave me a sense of the whole, a sense of the flock.

When I sat in the congregation, my field of vision narrowed. I was aware of myself and my family seated beside me. I was aware of the pastor who now stood in my place. But my sense of the church was radically changed. I still felt their presence, but anonymously.

I could see only the backs of their heads. Suddenly, I realized the extent to which my idea of what it means to be a church had been mediated through a particular line of sight.

We know the church is not the building. The true church is composed of "living stones" (1 Peter 2:5). But this does not mean that physical space is unimportant. Long before the first cathedral was ever conceived, when the first believers still met in homes, they did not entirely separate their identity from their physical surroundings. Paul sent greetings to Priscilla and Aquila and to "the church that meets at their house" (Rom. 16:5; cf. 1 Cor. 16:19; Col. 4:15; Philem. 2). He spoke of the church "in" Cenchrea, Corinth, and Asia (Rom. 16:1; 1 Cor. 1:2; 16:19).

I do not want to make too much of this. I am simply saying that, despite what we may say about the church building, we cannot avoid feeling some attachment to the space in which our encounters with God and his people occur. While it is theologically accurate to distinguish between the church and the building in which the church worships, it is pragmatically necessary to recognize the connection they share. Even those churches that deemphasize the importance of the building pay careful attention to physical space. They strip the building of religious trappings or rent a hall because of its location or functionality. Either way, they are acknowledging the importance of the space their church inhabits.

When Valley Chapel moved from its storefront to a new 5,000 square-foot building on Chapel Road, the same people took their places in the pews, but we were not the same church. Changing space altered the dynamics that affected the way we related to one another. A new building created a different context for our experiences together. We gained a great deal, but we lost something as well. In a sense, the church that existed on Main Street died and a new one was born.

Of course, the trouble with our attachment to physical space is that it easily becomes an idol. This is true even of ground that God himself consecrates as holy. In 701 BC the Assyrians besieged Jerusalem. They had already carried the northern kingdom into captivity, and Hezekiah pleaded with God to spare Jerusalem from a similar fate. The Lord replied, "I will defend this city and save it, for my sake and for the sake of David my servant" (2 Kings 19:34). Later, as the Babylonian threat loomed on the horizon, the people of Jerusalem convinced themselves this earlier promise was a permanent guarantee and that the presence of the temple protected them from divine judgment no matter how they lived (Jer. 7:4). They treated holy ground like a rabbit's foot, a lucky charm that protected them from God's judgment and from their enemies.

The Babylonians have faded into the dust of history, but our compulsion to preserve sacred space remains. In our case it is not a marauding army that threatens the gates but the prospect of change. The change may involve choosing a different color for the carpet or assigning rooms differently for the new Sunday school quarter. Either way, the experience is often traumatic.

One pastor described to me how his congregation nearly came apart at the seams when they considered tearing down their old building and putting up a new one. Half wanted to make the change, but the rest were content to remain in the old building. Eventually the issue became so contentious nothing would avert a major crisis. The pastor concluded that only an act of God could save them. He got his wish when a bolt of lightening struck the old church building and burned it to the ground. "It was the best thing that could have happened," he said.

God does not always settle matters so definitively. We are left to navigate our way through the complexities of sacred space without direct divine intervention. We do not mean to be idolaters, but we have given our hearts to these places. We feel reassured by their fading colors and frayed cushions. When the space changes, a part of our past dies in the process. When we leave it behind, we leave a part of ourselves there as well.

CHAPTER 19

My Hero

The little Baptist church where my brother attends looks like it is about a century old. It might have been plucked out of some rural town and set down on the outskirts of Detroit. The floor creaks under the weight of a handful of worshipers, and the sanctuary carries the scent of old wood mixed with a hint of mildew. The pastor, a middle-aged man with a drawl, works the crowd. He is joking with them and waiting for the service to start. The page numbers from the hymnal are posted on the wall, along with the number of worshipers in attendance.

On this occasion George is seated in the front pew next to his wife, Jan, looking like a nervous groom just before the wedding. He is about to be ordained and looks like he is having second thoughts. Ordination was the pastor's idea. George was reluctant, convinced that such things are reserved for those who possess greater gifts. He didn't think he was up to the challenge. I suppose he had good reason to doubt.

George seemed destined to travel a hard road from the womb. Being born is never easy. For my brother the slow journey from darkness to light was doubly difficult. Shortly after he was born, his lung collapsed. George survived, but at a cost. The lack of oxygen to his brain resulted in a learning disability. My brother didn't learn about his problem until he was in his thirties. By then he had suffered serious collateral damage, not only to the brain but also to the soul. He suffered multiple injuries. Some of them inflicted by my hand.

I was aware of none of this when we were growing up. I only knew George was my big brother. When the older kids bullied me on my way home from kindergarten, he was the one who rushed to my defense. Like all younger brothers, I trailed after him, watching his achievements with admiration and a touch of envy. George was the first to walk and talk. He always led in battle when we played army and was the chief architect when we built our backyard clubhouse. He was the first to get his own bicycle, the first to earn his own money, the first to drive, and of course, the first to go to school. It was in school that George first discovered he was different.

He couldn't read and had trouble writing after an accident damaged his right hand. After he was forced to repeat the first grade, officials at the school told my parents there was nothing they could do for him. They said it was unlikely he would ever learn to read. My parents found it hard to accept George's difficulties. Mother blamed the school. My father blamed my brother. George just thought he was dumb.

When school officials suggested my brother be placed in a special-education class, my parents refused to allow it. Perhaps they felt they were acting in my brother's best interests. There was a stigma attached to special-education classes in those days. The children who were sent there were social exiles in the eyes of their peers and were ridiculed as "retarded." But I suspect my parents' refusal had more to do with their inability to accept George's problem. They were convinced he could learn to read if the school made more of an effort. My mother was so certain of this, she decided to do the job herself.

This hardly sounds remarkable today, when homeschooling is a cottage industry with co-ops, consortiums, and major publishers providing resources for parents who want to teach their own children. But in those days it was a daring move. I'd never heard of a parent attempting such a thing. Teaching was for teachers, not mothers. My mother might just as well have announced that she was going to be our dentist or perform major surgery.

Her plan was audacious. She never finished high school. But mother was no dummy. She was well read and a lover of literature, especially William Shakespeare. She contacted the school to inquire about purchasing their old reading books. She made flash cards to teach my brother vocabulary. After she gathered her resources, she began to instruct my brother, sending him to class each day and then holding classes of her own when he returned home in the afternoon.

My sister, Lynn, and I were jealous of the attention being shown to our brother and demanded that we be allowed to participate. An already painful and often humiliating exercise was made worse for him by us. Too often we used the classes as an opportunity to show off our prowess in the areas he lacked. As if that weren't enough, my father decided the best way to motivate George was to ridicule him. The combination was toxic. George suffered through an endless cycle of failure at home and at school, mixed with liberal doses of verbal abuse. He couldn't understand why things that came easily to others were so hard for him to learn.

My father picked up an English paper of George's one night and started to berate him. The teacher marked my brother's spelling errors in unmistakable red. Seeing it, my father decided to add his own brutal critique. He cursed and began to badger my brother.

"What is this supposed to be?" he asked sarcastically. "You call this writing?" He read one of the misspelled sentences on the paper. It said, "Last night I had goog fesh for dinner."

"Goog fesh?" he roared adding an expletive. "What is goog fesh?"

Like a shark that has caught the taste of blood in the water, I sensed the ridicule in my father's voice and snatched the paper out of his hands. Looking at the barely legible handwriting with a smirk, I joined in. "It's supposed to say 'good fish,'" I jeered. "He can't even spell *fish*."

We continued to berate my brother, repeating the misspelled phrase over and over again as he suffered in silence. The bruised look in his eyes was the only evidence of our brutality. A strap could not have stung more. Though we never laid hands on him, we left a mark on his soul that remains to this day.

I have tried to explain my actions to myself many times. It was the result of my age. I was only a child. It was the result of my ignorance. I didn't know any better. I was a victim of bad parenting. I was only following my father's example. But I know better. I knew better even then. I lacked the vocabulary to name what I had done, but I knew it was sin. I was following in the way of Cain and Abel, Ishmael and Isaac, Jacob and Esau, following the path of sibling rivalry accentuated by sin. My words were meant to hurt.

Not long ago I asked my brother if he remembered the incident. Amazingly, he did not. But he vividly recalled the shame of his learning disability. "I just thought I was stupid," he said. "Sometimes I still feel that way." He always blamed himself. He never blamed us.

George's learning disability did not keep him from developing a strong work ethic. He was always the more industrious of the two of us. He earned money cutting lawns and got a job at a supermarket. By the time he was a senior in high school, he had saved enough to buy a white Dodge and spent his weekends tinkering on it. He installed special shocks that raised the car's tail end and made the vehicle appear to be charging forward even when it was standing still. He added a special muffler designed to boost the volume of the engine rather than reduce it. The rumble gave the impression of speed. He also nearly killed himself in it, careening off a light pole and traveling across several lanes on the expressway. When he came to, he and his passenger were lying amid shattered glass in the back seat. An inch either way, the police who wrote the accident report said, and he would have lost his life. It was not the last time God spared him.

When we reached our teens, George and I were bent on following different paths. We never shared the same taste in music or clothing. He was a "greaser" who slicked his hair back, listened to soul music, and liked to wear black. I was a "freak" who grew long hair, wore bell bottoms, and listened to acid rock. George wanted to join the army and serve in Vietnam. I was hoping to avoid the draft. I planned to go to college after high school. George was eager to finish so he could work more hours at the grocery store. For the most part the two of us kept to our own worlds.

Before long George was working so much I rarely saw him. He married a girl he met at the grocery store and went to work in an automobile factory. A few months later he came home from work early and found her with her lover. They were married for barely a year. "For the first time in my life I understood how a man could kill someone," he later told me.

Instead, he turned his back on them both and walked out the door. From that point on, George's life was marked by one setback after another. The automobile industry took a nosedive, and he was permanently laid off from his factory job. He lost the few belongings left to him after his divorce when his landlady set fire to the trailer in which he and his roommate lived. I occasionally worried about George and sometimes prayed for him. Mostly, though, I was occupied with my own affairs. We rarely saw one another. When he did drop by my house, he said little about his problems.

My wake-up call came one night when I awoke from a sound sleep with a sense of dread, compelled to pray for my brother. In particular, I felt impressed to ask God to spare his life. The longer I prayed, the more anxious I became, sensing George was in some kind of grave danger. I asked God not to let him die until he understood his need for Christ and put his faith in him. When I was done, I fell asleep and forgot about it.

A week later I got a phone call from my father. My brother's roommate contacted him saying George had tried to commit suicide. Despondent over his life, he slit his wrists with a kitchen knife. "He really meant business," my father said. "If his roommate had come fifteen minutes later, it would have been too late."

I asked when this took place, but I already knew the answer. It happened the night I couldn't sleep and felt impressed to pray. My brother's roommate discovered him about the same time I was asking God to spare George's life.

This was the point in his life when my brother did one of the most courageous things I have ever witnessed. He began the long dark climb out of despair. George started by asking for help. Counseling enabled him to understand how his background shaped the way he thought about himself. Medicine made it possible to cope with his depression. Perhaps most significant of all, the counselor gave George a book that explained the nature of learning disabilities.

George was astonished when he read the symptoms. "If I didn't already know what the book was about, I would have thought someone wrote it specifically about me," George said. Being able to put a name to his struggle gave my brother hope and made him think that maybe he wasn't stupid after all.

What George did next was even braver. With virtually no chance of being called back to work at the factory and with few job prospects, he went to my father, the same man who so brutally ridiculed him for being stupid as a child, and asked for financial help to go back to school. My brother explained that he wanted to become a respiratory therapist and needed to go to college. This time there was no ridicule or even skepticism. My father thought it was a good idea and agreed to pay for his schooling.

George's high-school grades posed a major hurdle in accomplishing this goal. Because they were so low, he first had to prove himself before the respiratory therapy program admitted him as a student. He also needed to find a job. In a bold attempt to overcome both obstacles, he enrolled in a program that trained him to be an emergency medical technician. But if this plan was going to succeed, George needed top grades in his first three courses, an impossibly high goal for someone whose high-school career was marked mostly by failure. An advisor at the school's learning center counseled him to buy the textbook for the anatomy and physiology course in advance and memorize all the bones in the body over the summer. George took him at his word and aced the course.

This became the pattern for all of George's classes. He bought the textbooks in advance and read them two or three times before taking the course. Once he was accepted into the program, he supported himself financially by working twenty-four-hour shifts as an emergency medical technician. He started out as a dispatcher and ended up as part of the ambulance crew, speeding through the shattered neighborhoods of inner-city Detroit. Sometimes he drove, but mostly he preferred to ride in the back with the patients. There was excitement behind the wheel, but it was when he was in the back that he felt he did the most good.

The surreal landscape of the inner city at night combined the horror of Dante's hell with the squalor of a third-world country. If the despair George felt during the worst point of his depression could have taken physical form, it might have looked something like this. Blasted neighborhoods still bore scars from the race riots of 1967. Crowded tenements, teeming with the poor, the elderly, and those who preyed on both, shared space with the smoke-scarred shells of burned-out buildings. At night the victimized and those seeking victims haunted the streets like apparitions.

George soon learned the tricks of the trade, how to put Vicks up his nose to block out the smell and how to handle patients when they were drunk or violent. He used caffeine to keep from falling asleep on the job and alcohol to take the edge off when he got home. He avoided the allure of amphetamines and never drank liquor while on the job.

When his shift ended George faced a more daunting challenge, going from the adrenaline rush of working the streets to the tedium of the classroom. He once told me, "When you work on the ambulance, you are working twenty-four hours on and twenty-four hours off. You are usually suffering from sleep deprivation." I asked him how he managed to keep up with school in the midst of it all. His answer was blunt, "I didn't sleep a lot."

In his classes George always sat in the first row. It helped him to pay attention. But some days the grueling schedule of the previous twenty-four hours took its toll. When George found himself nodding off in his anatomy and physiology class despite his best efforts to stay awake, help came from an unexpected source. The professor understood the challenges my brother faced with his learning disability, as well as the rigors of his job. He knew George needed an A in the class in order to be accepted in the program. In an act of grace, the professor sometimes ended class a few minutes early, when it was clear George couldn't keep awake any longer.

A stranger grace was at work as George rode the ambulance. Terrified by his daily encounters with death on the streets of Detroit, he began to think about God. He heard about God as a boy and even made a profession of faith as a child. But he did not seriously consider the implications of his decision until the chaos he encountered on the streets compelled him to reexamine what he believed.

"When you see enough people die," he later explained to me, "you have to look for an answer somewhere. Some people try to find it in drugs. Other people look for it in a bottle. I turned to God." The daily stress of making life-or-death decisions compelled him to look to something greater than himself for help. "When you screw up out there, people die," he said. "I just got to the point where I knew I couldn't make it without Jesus."

Still, George's movement toward Christ was slow and his growth gradual. Someone gave him a copy of Chuck Colson's biography. Colson's story impressed him with God's ability to change lives. After reading it George thought to himself, "If God can do that for someone like him, maybe he can do something for me."

The critical turning point came after he met and fell in love with Jan, the woman he eventually married. One holiday season he visited the tiny church where Jan's two sons were performing in the yearly Christmas program. The people in the church showed him love and were patient with his spiritual progress. "Sometimes I got off work, had a few drinks, and then showed up at church with alcohol on my breath," George admits. The people in the church accepted him as he was, and George saw something in their lives that was lacking in his. In time he recognized that what he felt was the need to have fellowship with Christ. George began attending the church regularly and started to read the Bible.

A week before my brother was to graduate from college, I had a vivid dream about the ceremony. In it my brother was dressed in a cap and gown and carrying his diploma with the Latin words *Cum Laude* inscribed on it. When he asked me what they meant, I laughed. "They mean 'with honors.' You graduated from college with honors."

I woke up the next morning and shook my head at the strangeness of the dream, chuckling at the thought of someone who barely made it through high school being able to graduate from college with honors. I decided the dream was merely a symptom of the guilt I felt over not being able to watch him receive his diploma. I put it out of my mind until the following week, when I received a phone call from my father.

"You're not going to believe this," he said. "You're brother graduated from college this weekend. He came up to me with his diploma after the ceremony and asked me why it had *Cum Laude* written on it."

There was a note of amazement in his voice. "Your brother graduated from college with honors and didn't even know it!"

George got a job working as a respiratory therapist in an inner-city hospital in the city of Detroit, where he discovered he preferred working in the emergency room for many of the same reasons he liked riding the ambulance. Saving lives was an almost daily occurrence there. George's faith added a new dimension to his work, as he combined prayer with the skills he learned in school and on the job. On Sundays he took attendance for the pastor, always adding one to the number he counted. I thought it was because he wanted to encourage the church's pastor. The church was small, with only a handful in the congregation each week. But my brother had a different reason, a theological one. "I did that because I figured God was there too," he explained.

George started visiting church members who were in the hospital and was eventually appointed a deacon. He continued his study of the Bible with an energy that put me to shame, even though I was a pastor. He applied the same diligence that helped him get through college, reading every book several times, including works of theology or commentaries.

All of this became the catalyst for a new dream that seemed even more impossible than his goal of becoming a respiratory therapist. It was no longer enough to save lives physically; he wanted to impact others on a spiritual level. George began to wonder how one became a chaplain for the fire department. After some preliminary investigation the results looked discouraging. Without a Bible college or seminary degree, the door was unlikely to open. George couldn't go back to school full time, and it took too long to complete a program attending part time.

Finally, my brother called the head chaplain at the Detroit Fire Department and learned he could volunteer as a chaplain's assistant. He began to read all he could find about the chaplaincy. His duties at the church also continued to expand, as my brother decided to try his hand at preaching. He progressed from chaplain's assistant to assistant chaplain and eventually full-fledged chaplain. His duties, I learned, were not much different from mine as a pastor. But George carried them out with more passion than most. George's difficult past became a storehouse of valuable experience, a training ground that even Bible college or seminary could not match.

This was the strange path that led to this moment, when George waits apprehensively for the elders of the church to gather around and lay hands on him. He frets with me about the magnitude of the responsibility and his unworthiness for the position. I tell him it is all a matter of grace, all the while knowing that I am the one who has been shown remarkable grace in this moment. I have been given the unexpected mercy of being able to call back the words I uttered so long ago when we were only children.

I tell the congregation that our paths, which once seemed so different, have converged over the years. We both have come to know Christ and we are both engaged in ministry to the church. We both preach. We are both ordained. My brother claims that I have accomplished the most between the two of us. But I know better. George's accomplishments outstrip mine. He has overcome more obstacles in the face of greater adversity without succumbing to bitterness.

He doesn't regret the difficulties he has faced. He doesn't see them as unfortunate twists of fate or himself as a victim of circumstance. He sees them as tools wielded by the gracious hand of God. "Without them," he says, "I wouldn't be the person I am today."

George doesn't consider any of his accomplishments remarkable. "I'm just a survivor," he says. "I'm no hero." Perhaps not to others. Certainly not to himself. But he is to me.

CHAPTER 20

Lover's Quarrel

After more than thirty years together, I fear she and I have grown cold toward one another. We are still bound by our old commitment, and neither of us has forsaken the other. But the meals we now share have more of an air of polite disregard than of pleasure. This was not always the case. There was a time when she was never far from my thoughts. When we were apart, I counted the days until I was in her presence again. I was patient with her shortcomings and charmed by her idiosyncrasies. Now, the best we seem to be able to do is to eye one another with a glare of disapproval.

Do not misunderstand me. We are still on speaking terms, she and I. But there is a note of censure in our exchanges. She doesn't think I am attentive enough. I am not as generous as I once was. I do not try hard enough to maintain our relationship.

For my part, I confess there is some truth to her complaint. I admit I often find her dull and unattractive. Like an old lover whose beauty has faded with age, she seems piqued and dowdy to me now. I sometimes harbor secret fantasies about leaving her behind. But I know I cannot.

I speak, of course, of my old mistress—the church.

I remember when I first sensed a change between me and the church. It was shortly after I left the pastorate to teach in a Bible college. I sat in the pew of an unfamiliar church with my family, no longer the minister but now a visitor. I listened to the buzz of the crowd and the low hum of the organ prelude. As the worship leader stepped up to the podium and invited us to stand and join together in a hymn, I felt a kind of exhilaration. I turned to my wife and gloated, "Just think, none of this depends on me."

As I settled in to listen to the message, I was soon distracted by the sound of restless movement and whispering nearby. I tried to put it out of my mind and pay attention, but the volume only increased. Scanning the pew to find the source, I was dismayed to learn the clamor was coming from my two boys. That was the point my youngest son decided to take a pencil out of the pew rack in front of him and launch it like a missile over the heads of the worshipers in the pew in front of us. I looked at my wife in astonishment.

"How can you worship with this racket going on?" I complained. She just laughed at my dismay. "Welcome to the pew!" she said.

As the service progressed I felt disoriented and a little bored. I felt like I should be doing something other than sitting. I tried not to critique the sermon but couldn't help noting points where I would have handled the text or the delivery differently. I came feeling self-conscious about the prospect of explaining that just a few weeks earlier I was the pastor of a church. I left feeling frustrated that nobody cared who I was or what I did. As far as I could tell I was invisible to the congregation.

Do not misunderstand me. People did not treat me rudely. The greeters at the door smiled and offered their hand. The people in the pew did the same when the pastor urged the congregation to turn to their neighbor and "tell them you're glad they're here." But it was rote, like the greeting you get from the flight attendant who stands at the cabin door and smiles with professional friendliness.

I am sure I didn't seem any friendlier to the church. During my years as a pastor I often "worked" the crowd on a Sunday morning, moving from pew to pew pressing the flesh and greeting the flock. When I spotted a new visitor, I made a beeline over to them to let them know they were seen and were welcome. When I visited with church members in their homes, I asked about their family or their health and commented on the weather. I even made the occasional remark about the local sports teams, whose track record was of little personal interest to me, in an effort to make conversation.

But these overtures did not come naturally to me. In a way, they were fueled primarily by professional ambition. It was my job to be interested. I wanted to succeed. I wanted the church to grow. Once I no longer felt personally responsible for making the visitors in the church feel at home, my social skills evaporated. Suddenly I felt awkward and tongue-tied in church. I didn't know how to start a conversation or what to talk about.

Not long after I returned to the pew, I greeted the pastor on the way out of church. He joked with me.

"Next week after the sermon we can trade places," he chuckled. "You can stand at the door and shake hands."

Instead of laughing, I choked back tears. For hundreds of Sundays I was the one standing at the sanctuary door with my hand outstretched. I smiled at the members of my congregation and exchanged greetings. The comfortable monotony of this weekly liturgy was broken only occasionally, like the Sunday I learned Joyce, a longtime member of my congregation, had cancer. She shook my hand with a dull smile and thanked me for the sermon. The detached look I thought I detected in her eyes turned out to be a glint of fear. A few minutes later Joyce's best friend, Sylvia, passed through the line and wept as she told me how the doctors discovered a spot on Joyce's lung the previous week. Joyce died a few months later.

On other Sundays eighty-year-old Elmer passed through the line. A member of the Methodist church down the road, he worshiped with us because his daughter Betty attended our church. Elmer usually sat near the front, slack jawed and drooping as he dozed through the message. Afterward he always shook my hand at the door and thanked me for the sermon. Elmer deviated from this script only once, after his daughter died unexpectedly, another victim of cancer. He fixed me with a haunted gaze, eyes still red from weeping, and asked, "Why didn't I die first?"

I assumed his question was rhetorical. But he didn't move on. Instead, he stood there, the dark circles under his eyes deepening as he gripped my hand and waited for my reply. I could only promise to pray for him.

Most of the time, though, the litany never varied. I stood at the door. The congregation passed by. We shook hands and recited the same words to each other. There was something reassuring about the empty phrases that passed between us, comfortable and dull, like the words of a familiar song.

That morning as I passed through the line and waited to shake hands with the pastor, their faces all came flooding back to me, our brief encounters now cast in a different light that made me blink back tears. I wished I could take my place once more at the door of my old church, like a shepherd standing at the gate, greeting the flock by name. I chuckled politely at the pastor's comment and shook his hand as I exited the church. Was I as perfunctory as this? I suspected I was.

I am not surprised to know some people are dissatisfied with church. I am surprised that it has happened to me. My perspective of the church changed after I stepped out from behind the pulpit and took my place in the pew. It didn't take very long before I realized I had become the kind of churchgoer I used to criticize as a pastor. I now evaluated churches in terms of what they offered me. Was the preaching interesting? Were there programs for my children? Did I enjoy the worship? I frowned on using such measures to evaluate the church when I was a pastor, partly out of fear that our small congregation failed to measure up. During my years in pastoral ministry my philosophy was, "Ask not what your church can do for you, ask what you can do for your church."

But the view from the pew was different. It did not seem unreasonable or selfish to expect the pastor's sermon to be interesting in exchange for my undivided attention. It was only natural to want programming for my children.

The sermon, too, sounded different on this side of the pulpit. Many of the admonitions I gave my congregation now came back to haunt me. Somehow they sounded hollow and self-serving on the lips of other pastors. I often reminded the church that my job was not to do the work of the ministry but to prepare God's people for that task. Yet when I heard these same truths on the lips of others, I felt scolded and suspicious of their motives. Were they really concerned about me as a person? Or were they only interested in what I could do for them?

Some of the pastors I met felt sorry for themselves and disappointed with their churches. They felt overworked and underappreciated. But I couldn't help wondering what they did during the week. To ask the question made me feel like a traitor. I disliked it when people in my church said such things with the implied accusation of laziness.

Were all pastors disillusioned with their churches? Like disappointed parents who perennially scold their children no matter what the grade, their sermons were spare in praise and tinged with chiding. As well as the church might have done, we could be doing better. We could always be doing better.

Was it really self-interest I detected in these pastors? Or did I merely attribute to them the motives which had plagued my own ministry? Determined to prove to myself that my sermons bore a different tone, I went to the file cabinet and thumbed through my old messages. I read them with the apprehension of a patient who has asked another doctor for an opinion when he already knows the diagnosis. After a few minutes I breathed a sigh of relief, permitting myself a self-congratulatory smile. These sermons weren't half bad. But as I read on, I grew less confident. I began to detect a shrillness in my messages, like a grace note suddenly gone wrong. It was the same tone I now found so grating in the sermons I heard in church. Was it them or was it me? I couldn't be sure.

My return to the ranks of the congregation was disorienting for others in the church too. I was no longer a pastor, but I wasn't quite a layperson. Some didn't know what to call me. Others weren't sure how to treat me. I suspected Sunday school teachers rolled their eyes whenever I showed up. In one class the instructor seemed unusually muddled as he tried to work his way through the lesson. I couldn't shake the feeling that he was eyeing me nervously but told myself I was being too self-conscious. Finally he stopped in midsentence, flushed red, and blurted out, "Dr. Koessler, what do you think?"

He meant it as a gesture of respect, but I was unnerved by the question with its suggestion that my opinion was the last word in all biblical matters. I soon discovered the fact that I taught in a Bible college gave added weight to anything I said. Class members regarded me as the resident expert on all matters pertaining to the Bible, whether I knew the answer or not. What is more, my remarks were often considered to be vested with the full authority of the Bible institute where I taught. This perception was almost as appealing as it was unsettling. My comments were no longer merely personal opinions. They were oracular pronouncements.

My natural shyness, combined with the uncertainty I felt about my changed role in the class, made me reluctant to say anything. I reserved my comments for points where I disagreed so strongly that I felt I could not be silent. This was probably not a good strategy. I came across as prickly and overly critical, especially since I was already prone to speak with a sonorous gravity which made every remark seem like a prophetic declaration. No wonder people in the class were polite but distant toward me.

Frustrated with our inability to connect with others in church, my wife and I decided we must not be trying hard enough. This was, after all, what I always suspected of those who found it difficult to make friends in my church. "A man that hath friends must show himself friendly," I intoned whenever someone suggested our little congregation was not as friendly as it could be.

While attending a church whose sign out front promised it was "the friendly church," my wife, Jane, and I were thrilled one Sunday evening when a couple invited us to go to a fast-food restaurant after the service along with two of their friends. The four of them spent the evening reminiscing about their summer vacations they spent together. They told us how close they were. They were best friends, closer than we could imagine. The implied message came through loud and clear: "Look elsewhere," they seemed to be saying. "This seat is taken."

Another church, whose members were genuinely cordial to us when we visited on Sunday morning, sponsored a church social at a pizza parlor. The event was intended to build "community" in the

Sunday school class. Unfamiliar with most of the members of the class, Jane and I walked into the restaurant feeling like a couple of teens attending their first middle-school dance. We considered sitting alone but decided to "show ourselves friendly" and chose a table already occupied by two other couples. As we sat down we tried to ignore the look of surprise on their faces. They asked us a few perfunctory questions, then continued their previous conversation with each other. We spent the evening listening with polite smiles and wondered why we came.

I once heard someone say every church is a friendly church, even when they aren't. "Everybody thinks their church is a friendly church," he explained. "Those who find it unfriendly leave." That is the trouble with friendly churches. They promise friendliness to newcomers but offer little in the way of friendship because the seats are already taken. Church members are satisfied with the relationships they have and aren't interested in finding more. Their dance card is full. They are happy to see you show up but expect you to find your own place.

Nearly two decades ago I watched my best friend slowly drift away from the church. The two of us met in college. I was impressed by his seriousness about the Christian faith and the way he was eager to share it with others. I could always tell where he had been during the day by the bread-crumb trail of gospel tracts he left across the campus.

A lover of books, my friend used his paychecks to purchase theological works and soon possessed a library that would be the envy of any pastor or professor. What is more, he actually read the books he bought.

He got involved in church, teaching in the adult Sunday school program and working with special-education students. But at some point my friend became frustrated with the church. The sermons were trite. The relationships shallow. Frustration gave way to cynicism, and it wasn't long before my friend stopped attending church altogether. Instead, he and a few friends decided to meet at a restaurant on Sunday mornings to discuss theology.

When he told me of his decision, I was disturbed. I couldn't understand how he could justify such a course of action. I told him that he and his friends were sinning and quoted Hebrews 10:25: "Let us not give up meeting together, as some are in the habit of doing, but let us encourage one another—and all the more as you see the Day approaching." But instead of being convicted, he was hurt by my response.

"I'm not forsaking the assembly," he explained. "My friends are Christians. We probably have deeper conversations about the Bible than most of the people at church."

For the next few years our relationship became increasingly awkward. Each time we met, my friend waited for the inevitable question. "How's your church life?" I asked, already knowing the answer.

"Why do we always have to talk about this?" he finally asked in exasperation. "Why can't you just forget about it?"

"Because I care about you too much to let it go," I said.

He was not convinced.

I spoke to him on the phone the other day, this time about my own struggle with church. I asked him why, after years of disillusionment, he finally decided to return to the pew. His explanation was simple.

"I got convicted," he said.

He was reading his Bible and came across Hebrews 10:25.

"It wasn't the 'meeting together' part that got me," he said, "so much as the part about the Day of the Lord. It seemed to be saying the closer we get to the Day of the Lord, the more I need the church."

He couldn't remember my quoting the same verse to him years earlier.

"I guess I still struggle with church," my friend admitted. "I tend to be critical. But I've decided to bite the bullet. I'm trying to help the people I come in contact with. I feel like a lot of people there are young in their walk with the Lord. There is an enthusiasm. They do a lot of charitable works there and their hearts are right. I'm going to stick it out and see what happens."

I hung up the phone feeling envious.

A colleague of mine once described her relationship with the church as a "lover's quarrel." Sometimes I think that would be an improvement for me. At least in a lover's quarrel there is passion. My relationship with the church feels more like a cold marriage, the union of a couple who still consort with one another, but only because they are obliged to do so. They have long since learned to live separate lives. If the church has been a disappointment to me, I am certain I am an equal disappointment to it. If I had returned to the pew a prodigal newly arrived in rags, I might have felt more welcome. Instead, I am more like the older brother, who labors up the path to find the house lit and the celebration already in progress. Disgruntled because the party is not for me, I linger on the threshold, unwilling to enter. My criticisms sound petty. My mood petulant. But in this story there is no father at the door, willing to plead for my patience. Only a stranger with a frozen smile and a limp handshake.

CHAPTER 21

Dangerous Worship

"The trouble with you all is that you are too white," **the** pastor declared in a booming bass voice. When the guest speaker in the chapel service of the college where I teach began his message with this rebuke, we all laughed in the self-conscious way people do when they aren't sure whether they have just heard a joke or an insult. Despite his words, the pastor wasn't really complaining about our school's ethnic makeup but about the style of our worship. Our worship, he seemed to be saying, was too formal. Too stiff. We didn't clap. We didn't smile enough. We needed to loosen up and be more expressive.

At first I was put off by his criticism. But as I thought about it, I wondered if he wasn't right. I am not comfortable with expressive forms of worship. I don't want to clap, or sway, or pump my fist in the air. Mostly, I want to be left alone. I don't want to hug my neighbor and tell him Jesus loves him. When I lift my hands in worship, it is usually to fold my arms. When I sing, I want to sit down. So maybe that pastor made a valid point. Perhaps my worship is too stiff and devoid of feeling. Maybe it is too formal.

But there are other times when I find myself in settings where the worship is more formal in nature, and I get the opposite impression. On those occasions the subtext of the service implies the opposite. My worship, those occasions seem to say, isn't dignified enough. It is too chirpy. Too simplistic. It is all heat and no light. My worship lacks history, theology, and depth. It has no dignity or solemnity. When I find myself in settings where the worship style is more high church than low, I worry such criticisms may be right as well.

Liturgical forms with their creeds and public confessions make me feel awkward. When the point comes in the service when the congregation must recite the Apostle's Creed from memory, and I realize the best I can do is the AWANA pledge, I feel ignorant and uncouth. But I don't want to seem crass, so I try to mumble the unfamiliar words and dutifully bow the knee. All the while feeling like I am watching someone else worship.

Not long ago I was asked to deliver the homily at a "traditional" worship service. At the point in the service when we were supposed to confess our sins, I forgot to kneel. Suddenly I felt a sharp tug, as the worship leader, who moments ago was standing next to me on the platform and was now on his knees, reached up and grabbed me by the jacket to pull me down.

This is often how I feel in worship, whatever the style. Pulled in one direction and cajoled in the other. Badgered until I comply with whatever form the worship leader thinks is consistent with "true" worship. It is as if I have been given a mask at the door of the sanctuary and am expected to put it on when the service begins. I cater to their demands in order to keep up appearances, but I am not sure I ever really worship.

Why do I find the church's worship so disappointing? What is it I want out of worship?

On hot summer nights in my childhood, I stretched out on the grass and gazed into the night sky. More aware of earth than heaven, at first I felt only the solidity of the ground beneath me, the pinprick sharpness of blades of grass, and the ticklish dance of a wayward ant on the back of my neck. At some point the ground seemed to fall away and the night sky filled my vision, until I felt as if I were caught up into the wide expanse of the heavens. This is what I want from worship—a sense of being swept up into something greater than myself.

I long for a sense of being on holy ground, the way I felt when I visited the Lutheran church where my sister attended parochial school. My parents took the whole family, but not willingly. They were shamed into the visit by my sister's teacher. Every Monday she asked those who attended worship the previous Sunday to stand. My sister was the only one who remained in her seat. When they could no longer bear her tears over this weekly embarrassment, my parents took us to church.

The place was so foreign I might have been a refugee landing on Ellis Island for the first time. The seats were hard. The preacher, like the Lord, was high and lifted up as he stood behind his large wooden pulpit. I knew none of the hymns. I could not understand the message; I could only listen to his voice as it thundered like the God of Sinai, certain that the light fixture above our heads trembled at the sound. Unable to participate in the liturgy, I huddled in the pew with my family and watched in bewilderment. I felt out of my element, like a guest who has stumbled into the wrong reception. Was it this sense of being out of place, in the presence of something greater than myself, that made it feel like worship to me?

There are moments when I wish I could return to those Saturday nights at the coffeehouse, where I learned my first songs of faith. They sounded more like campfire songs than hymns, with their rhymes and hand motions. My sense of God's presence was palpable then. I not only believed he was there with us, I felt it. I opened my eyes quickly after prayer, like a child awakening on Christmas morning, expecting to see God's glory receding in the distance.

I am too sophisticated for such worship now. I cling to the familiar, singing the songs I have already sung. I prefer the company of people I already know and like. The seats must be comfortable and the atmosphere bright. I want worship that is a reflection of me — my tastes, my preferences, and my personality. This is worship in my own image, the besetting sin of worship in a user-friendly age.

I am reserved and self-conscious in my worship. If I feel emotion, I am reluctant to show it. I dab the occasional tear away, but that is all. Most of the time, I do not feel much of anything at all.

I was struck by the contrast recently when I read of the worship of Mary of Bethany, who took a pint of expensive perfume, poured it on Jesus' feet as he reclined at dinner, and wiped his feet with her

of worship that helped our church grow numerically. Did it compare favorably to what other congregations were doing? Did it suit the market and attract people to our church? I suppose in some respects this is an improvement over the other approach. At least it considered the tastes of someone other than myself. But it was still a human-centered rather than a theocentric point of view.

Pragmatism was the lens through which those who reclined at the table with Jesus evaluated Mary's scandalous act of devotion. Judas considered Mary's worship to be a waste because he got nothing out of it. The others, taken in by Judas's masquerade, rejected it on more practical grounds. They were indignant because she did not put her expensive perfume to better use (Mark 14:4–5). Worship, they concluded, must be measured in the amount of good it does.

But they too missed the mark. This action of Mary was not intended to benefit anyone. It was a sacrifice of devotion pure and simple, a symbol of her love poured out at Jesus' feet. In human terms it was indeed a waste. It certainly did not help the others in the room to worship Jesus any better. If anything, it might have been a stumbling block to them, because it violated the customary rules of propriety. She who was neither wife nor sister touched Jesus, something no self-respecting rabbi permitted. Convention called for Mary to take her place alongside her sister, Martha, and serve. Instead, she took the role of a household slave. In a way, Mary was even lower than a servant, because a servant at least used a towel. Mary used her hair, which symbolized her glory as a woman. In a sense, she cast her glory at Jesus' feet.

This is familiar territory for Mary. Every time she appears in John's gospel, she is at Jesus' feet. But her act was still a waste. It did not help the others at the table to "see" Jesus any better. They missed the significance of her act. The benefit Jesus received from her action, if any, was minimal. Although Jesus praised Mary for what she did, she did not earn his favor as a result. He did not love her more because she used her life savings in this extravagance of devotion, and she was considerably poorer after it. If pragmatism is the measure of good worship, then Mary's worship was a failure.

This is often the case when I worship. It does not seem to do much good. I leave the worship service feeling dissatisfied rather than blessed. The worship is either too contemporary or too stodgy. Or else it is business as usual and I leave feeling much the same as I did when I came in. If we sing one song I like, I feel fortunate. The sermon sheds no new insight. My conversations with other worshipers never transcends the usual superficial observations about the weather or today's game. In short, as far as I can tell, nobody seems to receive observable or measurable benefit from the experience. There is no sense of divine presence, no moment of epiphany when I see the Lord in his glory. I register my presence and go home like a man who punches the clock.

Does this make it a waste? Perhaps the true value of worship cannot be calculated in terms of what we take away with us when we walk out the door. Marva Dawn describes worship as a "royal waste of time." It is not useful in the ordinary sense of the word. God does not need it nor does he gain anything from it. The only reason to offer it is because God deserves it.

I have asked myself what draws me most in worship. Why am I tempted to move from church to church like some kind of spiritual gypsy? What am I seeking? I like to think I am searching for a place where I sense the presence of God. But in truth it is the show I like. It is not the aura of the holy or the sincerity of devotion that attracts me. I am drawn to the circus as much as to the bread. I am attracted to the aesthetics of worship, the sound of the music, the atmosphere of the sanctuary, and the effect the experience produces in me.

This too is reflected in those who observed the worship of Mary of Bethany. The party is for Jesus, but these people have come for someone else. Many in the large crowd came because they knew Lazarus would be one of the guests. They wanted to see Jesus, but they were even more curious about the oddity of a man raised from the dead. This makes me wonder how often Jesus is only incidental to my worship. Is it possible the things I love most about worship have little to do with the object of my worship?

John Ortberg points out the danger of the circus when he speaks of worship which specializes in generating emotion by relying on methods that are shallow, artificial, and rarely reflective. He calls this "scarecrow worship," noting, "It would be better if only it had a brain."

This sounds like much of what I have experienced in "contemporary" worship. The music has the familiar comfort of a commercial jingle and the drama before the message the heartbreak of a three-minute soap opera. The sermon is relentlessly upbeat. There is no theological reflection. No exegetical content. No sense of the numinous. It feels as if the church has traded awe for cheap sentimentality.

I could turn to more traditional worship. These ancient rituals are solemn and mysterious. To some they are a refreshing change from the stark modernity and Madison Avenue glitter of contemporary worship. The sights, sounds, and smells of ancient worship seem more holy to those who have not been steeped in them all their lives. Is this because they are more holy or simply because they are unfamiliar?

The worship style of the high church has the advantage of coming from a tradition with more history and deeper theological reflection than its more contemporary counterparts, but it carries with it its own dangers. The familiarity of traditional worship is a bane as well as a blessing. The circus of contemporary worship may only have been replaced by a machine. Ask anyone who has been raised in a liturgical church, and they will be the first to admit it is all too easy to become mechanical and practice such forms by rote. The comfortable rituals to which we return week by week become empty and cold with time. The kind of worship that hides behind forms and uses exegesis and theological abstractions to keep the heart at bay is no improvement over scarecrow worship. "This is tin man worship," John Ortberg laments. "If only it had a heart."

I walk the knife edge between these two unhealthy extremes whenever I enter the sanctuary. Mary of Bethany, bowed in humility at Jesus' feet, shows me a third way. She strikes the perfect balance. Passionate and expressive in her worship, she is also theologically reflective. In his defense of Mary, Jesus made it clear that her action was prompted by a level of understanding about his mission that eluded the rest of the disciples. At this point she alone understood that Jesus came to die (cf. Mark 14:8). They accused her of being rash, but they were the ones who spoke without thinking. Of all those gathered at the table, only Mary was truly reflective.

Mary also understood the fleeting nature of worship. This was Jesus' defense when the others complained Mary was not being practical enough. Unmoved by their argument that the perfume she poured out in loving devotion to Christ could have been put to better use by being sold and the money given to the poor, Jesus took Mary's side. "You always have the poor with you," he told them, "and you can help them anytime you want. But you will not always have me."

Jesus' words remind me that the proper moment to express ourselves in worship may not be the most opportune. When it comes to my experience of the divine presence, God shows up whenever he pleases, with little regard for the calendar of worship or stated times of service. Mary's greatest act of worship occurred not in the synagogue or at the temple but at the dinner table. Like her, my most transcendent moments do not take place in the worship service.

Real worship is as ephemeral as a cloud of breath on a winter's day. I barely realize it has appeared when it begins to dissipate. The moment must be seized before it passes away altogether. I will have many opportunities to study, sing, or serve. But none quite like this. I may meet in the same place with the same people. It is likely I will observe the same order of service and sing the same hymns on another occasion. But this singular opportunity to express our devotion to Christ will have passed. Another may come that is equally meaningful, but it will not be the same.

This is the romance of worship. I never know when God will show up and stir me so deeply that I feel compelled to express myself in some extravagance of devotion. This is also the agony of worship, because in the meantime I must wait and battle with my competing desires for something to enjoy and for the service to do somebody some good. Despite my failure and disappointment, I return again and again to the place of worship. I enter casually, barely aware that I am treading on ground as dangerous as it is sacred. At any moment I may come face to face with the living God. Then, at last, I may find myself with Mary—on the floor at Jesus' feet. With all my pretense shattered, I will have nothing to offer except my naked devotion.

CHAPTER 22

The End of Home

Green Valley, the town where I served as a pastor, is not large.
It is the equivalent of only a few city blocks in length and width.
You could walk from one end to the other in a few minutes and
hardly be winded.

The town is bordered on the west by Route 29. If you take it
north for twenty minutes, you come to Pekin. Residents claim the
name alludes to the fact that one could bore through the earth and
come out on the other side in Peking, China. They are proud of
this geographical connection with Pekin's sister city on the opposite
side of the globe. So proud, in fact, that the high school originally
named its sports team the Pekin "Chinks." They were puzzled by
those who suggested that such a name might be insensitive at best
and possibly downright racist. To their credit, they eventually re-
moved this stigma while retaining their pride of location by renam-
ing the team the Pekin Dragons.

If you take Route 29 south for about an hour, you eventually
reach Springfield, the capital of Illinois. Abraham Lincoln was its
most famous resident. The little settlement where Lincoln began
to practice law is also close by. Springfield is the site of old Abe's
tomb. There is a bust of him near the entrance. If you rub his nose,
it is said, you will have good luck. Judging from the shine, many
visitors believe this to be true, but luck didn't count for much in the
area's economy during the years we were there.

It was a reflection of the hard times we were living through that
someone built a small apartment complex on the edge of Route 29

for those on public assistance. Longtime residents view its presence as something of a scandal, while those who move in and out of this complex are largely invisible to the rest of the community. One of the church's members told me people occasionally buy one of the many houses for sale in the town, move their families and possessions in, and then abandon the house when times grow hard. They just get in the car and go, leaving behind the house, the kids' toys, and all the furniture. No one knows where. This has happened often enough for the town to designate someone to go through its abandoned homes to inventory the property left behind.

The eastern edge of the town is marked by a large grain elevator and the railroad tracks that run near it. Every fall at harvest time the farmers' trucks line up to store their grain in the elevator. The grain elevator was the first landmark my oldest son learned to recognize as a toddler. After a long trip, when the elevator came into view, he realized we were almost at the end of our journey and cheerily piped, "Hooray, we're at the end of home!" But even though we were there nearly ten years, it never felt much like home to us. My wife, Jane, and I grew up near the city and lived in metropolitan areas most of our lives.

When I candidated at the church someone on the search committee asked whether I had a problem living in a rural community. "Oh no," I said. "We have cows just down the road from us where we live now." This was technically true. We were living in a small town that was really a suburb of Philadelphia. Until we moved to Green Valley, I didn't know what rural really meant.

Green Valley used to be a place, like the old Cheers bar, where everyone knew your name. This was still true to a degree when we lived there. During our first week there, my wife and I went for a walk down Main Street in town. A little girl saw us and grew wide eyed. As we came near, she started to back away from us. "Mommy," she said in alarm, "I don't know them." Judging from the way the adults sometimes stared at us, they felt the same way.

Some of the families could trace their presence in the town back more than a hundred years. When they spoke of one another, they identified themselves by family lineage. Listening to them was like reading the genealogies of the Old Testament. "That's Emma," one of the old-timers might say. "She was a Bergey, but then she married a Lindman." Then, as an afterthought, "Her mother's sister married my aunt's cousin." Those who said such things always outlined these complicated relationships in a tone which implied knowing the names was the same as knowing the faces. I, of course, was familiar with neither. My wife and I felt like outsiders all the years we lived there.

The main road through town, running east and west, is Toboggan Road. My father, who visited soon after we moved to the place, said the name must have been somebody's idea of a joke. A person needs a hill to use a toboggan, and Toboggan Road is as flat as could be. During winter the sun rose and set on that road. It is the road that runs past the house where we lived and the church where our congregation worshiped. It is the road on which my children, who were born after we moved there, rode bikes into town. It is the road I took when I went to visit the members of my congregation and the one I walked in the evening when I reflected on the strange paths in my life that brought me there.

I never intended to come to such a place. My arrival felt more like an accident than an act of God's sovereign will. In my senior year of seminary I sent out resumes hoping to find a church that might want me as their pastor. Valley Chapel was the only one that showed any interest. Was it divine direction or desperation that put me there?

I felt the same way about much of my Christian life, like someone on a journey who has been momentarily distracted from the trip by the scenery and has pulled over to the side of the road. Was this my destination, I wondered, or simply a stopping point along the way?

I realize now all points are merely stopping points, save one.

In the heart of town Toboggan Road is intersected by Church Street, so called because it runs past the Methodist and Presbyterian churches. Church Street used to connect to Route 29. Now it comes to a dead end near the cemetery. It is no longer a main thoroughfare, but everyone in Green Valley travels Church Street sooner or later. My first trip to the end of Church Street came when I was scheduled to speak at the town's annual Memorial Day service. This was a new experience for me. I had never celebrated Memorial Day before, except by attending opening day at the beach. The residents of Green Valley, however, take it very seriously.

They prepare for the event by decorating the cemetery. Fresh flowers are placed on the graves. Each veteran's grave has its own small flag, and a corridor of larger flags lines the cemetery entrance. The morning begins with a ceremony presided over by the local VFW. On that day each year they shoulder their weapons once again and march in solemn procession, albeit with a little less precision than in a younger day. A lone voice, weakened somewhat by age, calls the men to arms, and they honor the dead with a twenty-one gun salute. There is a brief moment of panic for me when it appears as if these venerable old men are pointing their weapons directly at the crowd.

They are, in fact.

But there is no real danger, since their guns are loaded with blanks.

After the ceremony the crowd mills about for a few minutes looking at the graves and making comments. Someone points out several of them to me, probably belonging to family members, and begins to run through the family lineage.

"To Enoch was born Irad: and Irad begat Mehujael: and Mehujael begat Methusael: and Methusael begat Lamech ..."

A little boy points out a large obelisk that marks one of the graves and observes, "Look, Ma, he must be the tallest man in here." Another person visits the mound that rises above the grave of one who has been newly buried, and I leave as soon as I am able.

The cemetery is where Betty Bussone now rests. Hers was the first funeral I ever performed as a pastor. A vitamin enthusiast and an avid reader of health magazines, her death at a relatively young age was a shock to the church. I was terrified at the prospect of performing her funeral, afraid I would do or say something foolish. I envisioned myself tripping over the coffin and watching it tumble to the floor or forgetting her name. None of these things happened.

Joyce Reining, a woman who sang in our church choir, came to me after Betty's funeral and said, "That's the kind of funeral I want you to do for me." I muttered something about that day being a long way off. Ironically, Joyce's words proved prophetic. Her funeral was one of my last official acts as pastor of Valley Chapel.

Harry Koch is also buried in the cemetery. He died after I left the church to become a college professor. Harry served on a mine-sweeper while in the navy and was the principal of the high school for many years. He was a gruff sort who always frightened me a bit. He was the only person I ever met who actually read the articles in *National Geographic*. He read every issue from cover to cover.

The cemetery is where seven-year-old Tyler Hall was laid to rest. Tyler died on a Sunday morning. I got the call just after the service ended. There was an accident. Tyler had been hurt. I was needed right away.

I took Route 29, barely noting the cemetery, and arrived at the emergency room just as they were wheeling Tyler in on a gurney. The paramedics looked grave and his parents were beside themselves. Tyler's mother watched the life drain out of her son while she held him in her arms.

For the next few hours I stayed with Tyler's parents in the emergency room and tried to offer comfort as friends and family members arrived. A few attempted to make sense of what happened to the couple. One old man, an uncle perhaps, intoned through his tears, "God never gives us more than we can bear. The reason he let this happen to you is because he knows you are stronger than most. Someone else might not have been able to bear it."

They didn't look strong to me.

Before long the hospital chaplain arrived on the scene. She listened as Tyler's parents asked no one in particular why such things happen. She didn't try to answer the question for them.

I stayed until they told me to go, and on the way out I asked myself why I ever wanted to be a pastor. I had little to offer, a compassionate touch and a prayer, perhaps, but nothing strong enough to assuage this kind of pain.

A few days later one of the workers in our children's program came to see me. I was thinking about the tragedy and wondering whether my being a pastor was making a difference. "John, I thought you would want to know something Tyler said to me last week," she told me. She said Tyler came to see her on the last day of vacation Bible school after the meeting and asked her to pray with him. Tyler said he had accepted Jesus as his savior before but just wanted to make sure.

The accident was the next day.

A few weeks after the funeral, Tyler's father visited our church. Not usually a churchgoer, he came to show appreciation for what our church did for his family. I was humbled by his gesture. As far as I could tell, we did very little for him. We wept with him, prayed for him, and tried to point him to God. But we could not remove the greatest stumbling block that kept him from embracing our faith. We could not tell him why God permitted the death of his son. Like so many other visitors, he attended our church for a few Sundays and then stopped.

On my last Memorial Day in Green Valley I visited Tyler's grave. Someone had placed a small toy car on it in his memory. It sat on the stone, next to some flowers, like an offering. I pictured his face and tried to recall the faces of all the other children who passed through our programs down through the years. How many of them came to know Christ? How many, like me, started on a spiritual journey that continued long after they left us? How many simply disappeared from view?

I thought about Beulah Baptist at the other end of Church Street in the town where I grew up. Like Tyler and the other children in our programs, I visited there a short time and moved on, barely noticed by those who called the church home. I was one of hundreds who passed through the church's doors and were eventually forgotten. I do not blame the church for this. I did not stay long enough to make an impression. Beulah was only a stopping point for me on a longer journey. There was no reason for them to remember me. I remember Tyler only because of his traumatic death. Had he lived, I suspect I would have forgotten him, just as I have forgotten the names of most of the children who attended our programs. We are all transients, quickly forgotten, and at some point whatever road we are on, like Church Street, inevitably comes to a dead end near the cemetery.

Ten years after we lived and ministered in Green Valley, our family passed through the town on a vacation trip. We came to the grain silo at the edge of town and reminded our son Drew how, when he was little, he would cheer at that point in the trip and say, "We're at the end of home!" We drove past Minnie's place, with the little building next door where our congregation used to meet, and past the parsonage lawn where we watched the walls go up on the new church building. My boys said they were more comfortable living in the country than in the city. Jane and I confessed that we were never comfortable there. It never felt like home. But then, I don't know of any place that does.

When we passed the cemetery, I thought again of the people in my old congregation who are buried there now. I imagined Tyler's grave, now covered with the grass of several seasons, and wondered if the toy was still there.

I wondered if my boys might one day come back to Green Valley to live. Would they find wives, settle down, and attend church? And would they, someday long after I am gone, also make the trek to the end of Church Street and take their final rest there?

It would be all right if they did. Sooner or later everyone travels Church Street. When it comes into view, you know you are almost home.

Acknowledgments

I am grateful to many people for this book. Mark Sweeney, my agent, not only was a strong advocate in presenting this to the publisher, he helped me to think through the book in the early stages. Mark, you have been God's blessing to me, serving alternately as advisor, coach, cheerleader, and friend. This is a much better book because of your counsel.

I probably would not have written this book if Mark Tobey had not encouraged me three years ago to explore the genre of personal narrative. Thank you, Mark, for pushing me in a new direction. My former colleague Billie Sue Thompson also was a tremendous encouragement to me. Chapter 7 is for you, Billie Sue!

I am thankful for the interest of Agnieszka Tennant, Mark Galli and the folks at *Christianity Today,* as well as that of Marshal Shelley and those at *Leadership.* Your interest in my writing helped others to see the potential for this project.

I owe a special debt of appreciation to Jamie Janosz, my colleague at Moody Bible Institute, who read the manuscript and did a preliminary edit. I am also particularly appreciative of Christine Anderson's suggestions and the editing of Brian Phipps. The writing is much stronger as a result of their work.

I feel privileged to be published by the excellent folks at Zondervan and am particularly excited to be working with Paul Engle again. Thank you, Paul, for your gracious way and encouraging words.

Of course, I must also thank my wife, Jane. She is the love of my life, my first editor, and my best critic. Thank you, Jane, for telling me so often that writing is never a waste of my time. Thank you for living through half of my life's story and listening repeatedly to the other half without growing weary. Or, at least, without letting on that you were weary of hearing it.

Last, but certainly not least, I must express my gratitude to God and his Son, Jesus Christ. Telling my story has helped me to see your hand upon my life in a new way. I am thankful to be your child.

hair (John 12:3). There is a kind of nakedness in her devotion that scandalizes everyone in the room. Everyone, that is, but Jesus.

Judas objects to Mary's act, arguing that it is a waste of good perfume. It should have been sold, he complains, and the money given to the poor. Imagine what good could have been done with the proceeds, which amounted to a year's worth of wages. His argument is reasonable enough to persuade the others at the table. But Judas is being disingenuous. He is a man in a mask. Judas doesn't care about the poor. He doesn't care about propriety. For that matter, he doesn't care about Jesus. Judas is a thief who steals from the treasury, and he has just seen a year's worth of income that could have lined his pockets poured out on the floor.

Mary's act is meant to stand out in bold relief against the duplicity of Judas. I find I need the scandal of her naked devotion because it challenges me to strip away my own pretence in the presence of Christ. When Mary comes to worship, she leaves her mask at the door.

Like Judas, I too am inclined to be a thief when it comes to worship. More often than not, my preferences in worship do not take God's interests into account but only my own. It is worship for my sake rather than his. I suppose this is not entirely wrong. Theologian Donald Bloesch has noted, "Proper self-concern is not excluded from the worship experience, but it is always subordinated to the glory of God and the wonder of his love." My struggle is in knowing what constitutes proper self-concern. Is it too much to want to enjoy the music? Is it unreasonable to hope that the sermon holds my interest?

Yet I am not sure how to tell when proper self-concern has become self-absorption. I calculate the value of what others do in worship in terms of what it means for me. If I "got something" out of the service, then it was good worship. If not, then it was lame. God and the rest of the congregation are left out of the equation. I worry that my measure of what constitutes good worship is really just narcissism.

When I was a pastor I judged the church's worship from a more utilitarian perspective. I wanted the congregation to practice a style

We want to hear from you. Please send your comments about this book to us in care of zreview@zondervan.com. Thank you.

ZONDERVAN.com/
AUTHORTRACKER
follow your favorite authors